BEYOND WELCOME

Previous Books by the Author

The God Who Sees: Immigrants, the Bible, and the Journey to Belong

BEYOND WELCOME

Centering Immigrants in Our Christian Response to Immigration

KAREN GONZÁLEZ

BrazosPress
a division of Baker Publishing Group
Grand Rapids, Michigan

Published by Brazos Press
a division of Baker Publishing Group
PO Box 6287, Grand Rapids, MI 49516-6287
www.brazospress.com

Printed in the United States of America

Library of Congress Cataloging-in-Publication Data
Names: González, Karen (Karen J.), author.
Title: Beyond welcome : centering immigrants in our Christian response to immigration / Karen González.
Description: Grand Rapids, Michigan : Brazos Press, a division of Baker Publishing Group, [2022] | Includes bibliographical references.
Identifiers: LCCN 2022004873 | ISBN 9781587435607 (paperback) | ISBN 9781587435867 (casebound) | ISBN 9781493438419 (ebook) | ISBN 9781493438426 (pdf)
Subjects: LCSH: Emigration and immigration—Religious aspects—Christianity. | Hospitality—Religious aspects—Christianity.
Classification: LCC BR115.E45 G66 2022 | DDC 261.8/38—dc23/eng/20220302
LC record available at https://lccn.loc.gov/2022004873

The author is represented by the literary agency of Gardner Literary, LLC, www.gardnerliterary.com.

The names and details of the people and situations described in this book have been changed or presented in composite form in order to ensure the privacy of those with whom the author has worked.

Baker Publishing Group publications use paper produced from sustainable forestry practices and post-consumer waste whenever possible.

22 23 24 25 26 27 28 7 6 5 4 3 2 1

• • •

In memory of my Tía Mocle,
Thelma Elizabeth Ramos Mortley,
who fought the good fight
and now rests with our ancestors
and in the presence of God

• • •

Contents

Introduction

The ideas in this book were born en conjunto—that is, in community with many other people in my life, mostly my Latina friends, my comadres. Together we discussed what to call ourselves in English because English is a language in which nouns and adjectives do not have a gender. We discussed Latino/a, Latine, and Latinx as possibilities. I struggled with how to name our community because I know there is power in being able to name ourselves.

I am aware that there is disagreement about what exact term to use to reference our community, and I have heard and understand the objections to all of the terms. In the end, words are imperfect, but they are all we have, and I had to choose.

Ultimately, I chose the word "Latinx" (pronounced lah-teen-equis) for a few different reasons. First, I appreciate the way that *x* references an unknown factor, as it does in algebra. Our community is difficult to define because we come in all races: white, indigenous, Asian, Black, and mixed. We also come from so many countries that though we may speak Spanish, our cultures are distinct. In addition, we are still defining ourselves within the North American context; we are changing the culture, but it is also changing us. Finally, I appreciated the way the word "Latinx" is genderless and, thus, inclusive of my siblings in the LGBTQ+ community.

Throughout this book, I also use different terms to discuss human flow. It is important to define them for the reader:

Migrant: Any person who relocates within their own country from one state or province or region to another, permanently or temporarily.

Immigrant: A person who leaves their home country and moves to another country permanently.

The only difference between a refugee claimant and an asylum seeker is *where* they apply for their status. The following definitions come from the United Nations as well as US law:

Refugee: Someone who is unable to return to their country of origin owing to a well-founded fear of being persecuted for reasons of race, religion, nationality, membership of a particular social group, or political opinion. Refugee claimants apply for and receive the status *before* they arrive in their country of resettlement.

Asylee: Someone who is unable to return to their country of origin owing to a well-founded fear of being persecuted for reasons of race, religion, nationality, membership of a particular social group, or political opinion. Refugee claimants apply for and receive the status before they arrive in their country of resettlement. Asylum seekers apply for their status *at* a US port of entry or *after* they are already admitted to the US.[1]

It is my hope that defining these terms will bring clarity to you as the reader. I hope this book will be helpful to you as you seek to love your neighbors as yourself.

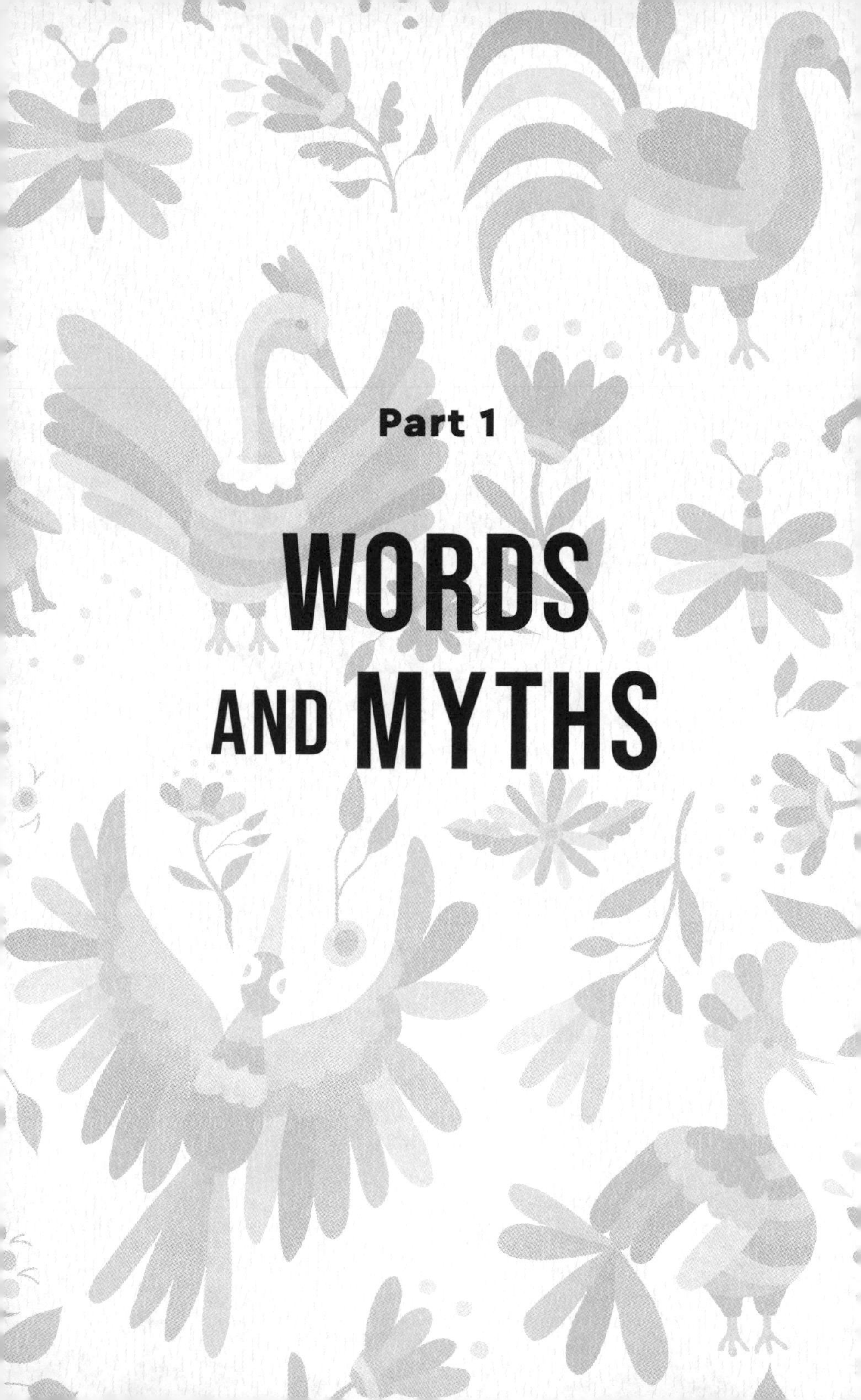

Part 1

WORDS AND MYTHS

Strangers in a Strange Land

The Myth of Assimilation

Donde fueres, haz lo que vieres. (Wherever you go, do whatever you see.)

—Latin American proverb

"Nunca te olvidaremos"—we will never forget you—was emblazoned on the T-shirts of nearly all the middle school Mexican girls. The words were written in perfect script and were positioned above a picture of a smiling Selena Quintanilla, who was looking out with her signature dark, wavy locks. It was 1996, and I was a first-year teacher at a middle school just east of Tampa, Florida. Most of the students who looked like me were children of migrant farmworkers; their parents came to town for the winter harvest and moved on at the end of the season. The Tejana singer Selena Quintanilla, known simply as Selena, had died the year before, and the community still listened to her music and mourned her loss, proclaiming on their T-shirts that she would never be forgotten.

I am now ashamed to admit it, but I cringed whenever I saw one of the T-shirts. I was one of two brown Latinx teachers in the entire school, and there was open hostility toward the mostly Mexican farmworkers in the city and, by extension, toward their children. They were poor and lived in trailer parks, were not permanent residents, and didn't seem to want to assimilate into the wider American culture by speaking only English. Didn't these kids understand that our language and culture could be private, reserved for the comfort of our families and homes? By day we could be part of the mythical melting pot, blending into the white American culture of the school; by night we could be fully ourselves: sing our Selena songs, eat our spicy food, and speak our mother tongue. Nevertheless, the kids never failed to greet me in Spanish in the hallways even though I always responded in English. As much as I wanted to distance myself from them in an effort to belong, my brownness made me one of them, and they never let me forget it with their playful familiarity.

Nobody taught me to assimilate to the white-dominant culture of the US, but I unconsciously adapted as a survival skill; life became easier when I erased parts of myself and revealed only the parts that fit in with the culture's comfort level and expectations. When I spoke Spanish to my cousin at a high school football game, angry fellow students yelled, "This is America! Speak English!" So I did—I was angry, but I became much more cautious about speaking my heart language publicly. When white classmates returned from Christmas vacation, boasting of trips to California or the mountains of North Carolina, I did not share about our family Christmas in Guatemala with marimbas and fireworks. And when a white friend laughed hysterically at Howard Stern playing Selena's music alongside a track of gunshots while Stern mocked her death, her music, and her fans, I pretended I found it amusing too.

My white colleagues asked me about what they called "the woman" T-shirts. I explained quickly who Selena was and then changed the subject, but they were interested and perplexed by the prolonged public mourning. I knew I could not make them understand what the loss of a brown Tejana singer with a curvier body meant to brown immigrant girls who are used to seeing fair-haired waifs with light eyes starring on American television shows as well as on their favorite telenovelas. On Spanish network television, women who look like Selena are often relegated to minor roles as maids and only appear in the background; they look down, take orders, and reply submissively, "Si, señora." That is a fact even today, more than twenty-five years after Selena's death. Selena represented something beyond herself; seeing her was dignifying in a way I could not articulate at the time. It meant that we—the Spanglish-speaking, curvy brown girls—could be the leading ladies, could be centered and recognized just as we are.

Those tender feelings and that ethnic pride were private. Publicly, I was embarrassed because I wanted the other teachers to see me as one of them: a fellow American teacher who shared their language, culture, and professional skills. I constantly heard grumblings and complaints about the Mexican students. One school leader, a self-professed Christian, called the Mexican boys "RDBs" in code over the walkie-talkies that the school administrators used. I later learned that RDB was shorthand for "regular dirt bag." Many adults working at the school whispered about the "inappropriate" clothing the Mexican girls wore: "Where are their parents? Who lets them dress like prostitutes?" Never mind that the white boys and girls behaved and dressed similarly.

Given this hostile environment, I wanted nothing to do with being different, with being seen as the brown Guatemalan immigrant I am. I did not want to be connected to the scantily clad or the dirt bags. All I wanted to do was blend in and disappear, something the kids and apparently my colleagues did not understand.

Hunger of Memory

The first time I read anything by a Latinx writer was in college. In my nonfiction creative writing class, we read *Hunger of Memory: The Education of Richard Rodriguez* by the Chicano writer Richard Rodriguez. The book is a memoir of Rodriguez's educational journey in Northern California as a child of Mexican immigrants. I was twenty-one at the time and inspired—in all the wrong ways.

As I understood it, Rodriguez talked about the immigrant experience as one that necessitated assimilation, and that assimilation was costly because it required alienation from your past, your family, and your culture of origin. That's just the steep cover charge we immigrants have to pay to enter the club of higher education, middle-class America, and upward social mobility.

The book is beautifully written and contains very poetic prose. But whether Rodriguez intended it or not, the central idea I absorbed was that immigrants could choose to assimilate or live in failure outside of mainstream culture. This false dichotomy stayed with me and influenced my own identity formation as well as my teaching philosophy with Black and brown students.

My job, I told myself, is to help my students assimilate into the mainstream in order to be successful. I recognized, as Rodriguez did, that there would be losses for them in this venture and that was not fair, but it is what success required. We just play the cards we are dealt, and these are our cards. End of story.

In my fifth year of teaching English, we received new textbooks, and I was annoyed at the exclusion of the classics in favor of "diverse authors." All "diversity" meant to me was having to rewrite lesson plans that I had spent years painstakingly perfecting and giving up treasured stories and novels in favor of more contemporary ones in order to appease some politically correct school board members. The fact that my Black and brown students and I were not represented in the old curriculum never bothered me. There is no room or value for representation when assimilation is the goal, because assimilation means that we are all absorbed into a whole where no one is supposed to be different.

One day I was in my classroom after school preparing a lesson on a narrative poem by the Puerto Rican writer and educator Martín Espada. The poem, "Tony Went to the Bodega but He Didn't Buy Anything," is about a disadvantaged Puerto Rican boy who lives in a predominantly Latinx neighborhood in New York City and eventually leaves the neighborhood for law school in Boston. There, he curses the cold spring and misses the smells and people of his old neighborhood. The poem describes the loneliness and alienation he experiences in this new environment where nobody looks like him.

He walks the neighborhoods in search of any semblance of home and arrives at a bodega, a small Latinx grocery store, where he goes in but does not buy anything. He just hangs out, content to be around people who are brown like him and who speak Spanish. When he finishes law school, he decides to open his law practice above the bodega, among his own people whom he will serve with his professional skills, and he is happy at last.

I remember sitting in my classroom by myself, and I just started crying—I found that poem so poignant and hopeful. I often told students that literature could move us, but I had not experienced it myself in this way. I had never considered the possibility of another way—of being an American without losing my cultural and ethnic identity.

Strangely, this idea had never even presented itself as a possibility in the church. We talked so much about our identity in Christ, and yet all our leaders, authors, and theologians were white men. Never was I even given a framework for considering my own experience as different and in need of processing. In all our conversations about racial reconciliation, not once did I hear a Christian leader suggest that I would experience God differently through my gender, culture, and language—that God would meet me as an immigrant woman of color. In fact, looking back I see that though these leaders meant well, our conversations never amounted to much except to make white Christians feel better without having to give up power or be uncomfortable.

While I still believe that Rodriguez's book has value because it is his story, the way that I internalized his views was harmful as I was striving to form my identity as an immigrant woman of color. It also deeply affected me as a teacher of color. I inflicted this same perspective on my Black and brown students, and I now regret the way I harmed them by telling them in direct and indirect ways that success meant giving up their ethnic and cultural identities too.

The Story of Zaphenath-Paneah

Assimilation is a key component of colonizing both lands and people. Moreover, it has been historically required for survival for many immigrant people, not just those we know personally but even those we meet in the pages of the Bible. Joseph in the book of Genesis is the most prominent example that comes to mind.

I have loved this story since encountering Joseph's words in Genesis 50:20: "Even though you intended to do harm to me, God intended it for good, in order to preserve a numerous people, as he is doing today." This verse encapsulates how Joseph makes sense of his own suffering. He endures the worst treatment at the hands of his brothers—they intend to murder him but instead separate him from his father and sell him to slave traders headed for Egypt. There he experiences not only enslavement but also incarceration for a crime he did not commit. He suffers cruelly for thirteen years. He leaves Canaan as a naively arrogant seventeen-year-old and is reunited with his family when he is well into his late thirties. It is noteworthy that he does not return to Canaan when he is set free; his lost family comes to Egypt in search of food during a famine, and they inadvertently find each other.

However, his story seems to end well—so well that most of us only see Joseph's resilience and leadership gifts. After interpreting Pharaoh's dreams correctly, Joseph helps him and all of Egypt to prepare for the coming famine that will follow seven years of plenty. Pharaoh rewards him: Joseph is dressed in the finest clothes, given power that makes him second only to Pharaoh, and provided an Egyptian wife. Scripture says, "Pharaoh gave Joseph the name Zaphenath-paneah; and he gave him Asenath daughter of Potiphera, priest of On, as his wife. Thus Joseph gained authority over the land of Egypt" (Gen. 41:45). Joseph is even renamed—no longer Joseph but Zaphenath-paneah, an Egyptian name that reveals his fully assimilated identity as an Egyptian.

Nonetheless, we readers are aware that Joseph is not *really* an Egyptian. He is a son of the great patriarch, Jacob, whose father was Isaac and whose grandfather was Abraham; he belongs to the people of Israel, the Hebrews who are God's chosen people.

But it is worth considering: Is he *really* still strictly a Hebrew?

He has been in Egypt longer than he had ever been in Canaan; Egypt is where he spent his young adulthood and matured into middle age. He speaks the language and understands the culture, even speaking to his own brothers incognito through an interpreter (Gen. 42:23); he marries a local woman; and he communicates freely with Pharaoh as his second in command, instructing his own brothers as to what to say and do to get to the land of Goshen (46:28–34). No mention is made of the need for a translator or a cultural attaché to help him navigate life in Egypt. Even when he gains freedom and power, he makes no effort to return to Canaan. He uses his wisdom and leadership not to bless the people of God, his own people in Canaan, or even the world at large, but strictly to prosper in his adopted country.

Some of us might make sense of Joseph's actions by blaming God. We may conclude that God kept Joseph in Egypt to save and bless all the nations. This is all part of God's cosmic plan that Joseph knows nothing about yet. But this interpretation, however much it might make sense of and simplify a complex story, also robs Joseph of agency. God is not the great puppeteer in the sky—Joseph has options, and God is certainly powerful enough to accomplish plans with and in spite of Joseph's choices. We also know from Joseph's later actions that he deeply loves his father and his younger brother, Benjamin. Why does he not return for a visit? Does he not wonder how his biological family is faring in Canaan? Would it not be prudent and kind to at the very least notify them that a famine is coming and that they should prepare? Why does he not send for the family he lost, even just his father?

The text does not answer these questions, but it is fair to assume that for his own survival, Joseph fully assimilated to life in Egypt. Essentially, he was now an Egyptian. Old Testament scholar Walter Brueggemann posits that Joseph aligns himself with Pharaoh and helps his adopted country to establish a "food monopoly."[1] Then, as now, tyrants weaponized food and used it to control hungry people; Joseph assists Pharaoh in these endeavors. Brueggemann goes on to exegete the incidents in Genesis 47:13–26:

> The [Egyptian] peasants, having no food of their own, come to Joseph, now a high-ranking Egyptian, and pay their money in exchange for food, so that the centralized government of Pharaoh achieves even greater wealth [v. 14]. After the money is all taken, the peasants come again and ask for food. This time Joseph, on behalf of Pharaoh, takes their cattle [vv. 15–17]. . . .

> In the next year, the third year, the peasants still need food. But they have no money and they have no livestock. In the third year they gladly surrender their freedom in exchange for food.[2]

Even Brueggemann refers to Joseph as an Egyptian, not as a Hebrew, perhaps because only a fellow elite Egyptian leader would create the economic conditions in which the Egyptian peasants give up their freedom and their land. They cry out to Joseph,

> "Shall we die before your eyes, both we and our land? *Buy us and our land in exchange for food.* We with our land will become slaves to Pharaoh; just give us seed, so that we may live and not die, and that the land may not become desolate." *So Joseph bought all the land of Egypt for Pharaoh.* All the Egyptians sold their fields, because the famine was severe upon them; and the land became Pharaoh's. As for the people, he made slaves of them from one end of Egypt to the other. (Gen. 47:19–21)

We do not often note this part of Joseph's story; most of us are infinitely more comfortable discussing God's providence in his narrative, his rise from slavery and imprisonment to leadership and glory. According to Brueggemann, the enslavement of Egyptians and later the Hebrews occurs "by the manipulation of the economy in the interest of a concentration of wealth and power for the few at the expense of the community."[3] And all of it was Joseph's doing; he was the right hand of Pharaoh that unwittingly ended up becoming the instrument by which not only the Egyptians but also he and his family's descendants are enslaved. The supreme irony often lost on all of us is that Joseph created a system of exploitation so brutal that God raised up another young Hebrew named Moses a few generations later to free the people from bondage.

It is fascinating to read Joseph's story from this perspective—one that recognizes that Joseph probably did not see himself as a Hebrew or even a global citizen but as a fully assimilated Egyptian. It makes me wonder whether he felt pressured to prove his Egyptian-ness the way so many of us immigrants feel pressured to prove our American-ness or Canadian-ness. Perhaps he still spoke Hebrew, and his Egyptian had a strong accent. Perhaps he worried that his neighbors might question his allegiance to Egypt and overcompensated by assimilating to systems of oppression to avoid the whispers and suspicions. How might this story have turned out differently if Joseph had held on to his Hebrew identity and culture but integrated into Egyptian culture? Would he have sought the common good instead of only what was good for Pharaoh?

Moses In-Between

It is not appropriate to judge Joseph by twenty-first-century standards, but it is notable that there are characters in the Bible who made different choices when caught between two cultures. Moses, for example, had a similar experience to Joseph in that he was a Hebrew person who grew up among Egyptian people, though in more favorable circumstances.

Those who have watched Cecil B. DeMille's *The Ten Commandments* will be familiar with Moses's origin story: to a people oppressed and subjugated is born a baby boy. However, Pharaoh has ordered that all baby boys be murdered (Exod. 1:22), so his mother, Jochebed, puts him in a basket in the river, hoping to save him. He is saved! Not only is he saved, but he grows up in the palace as the son of Pharaoh's daughter. Moses's life is one of privilege—he lives among the elite of Egypt, but he cannot ignore what he sees happening to people who are just like him: "One day, after Moses had grown up, he went out to his people and saw their forced labor. He saw an Egyptian beating a Hebrew, one of his kinsfolk. He looked this way and that, and seeing no one he killed the Egyptian and hid him in the sand" (2:11, 12).

Moses flees to Midian to escape the consequences of this murder. He leaves behind his life of privilege and wealth and starts a new life as a fugitive, even marrying and starting a family. In this new land, Moses calls himself the Hebrew word for "stranger" or "foreigner." Writer and theologian Daniel José Camacho wonders if perhaps Moses felt like a stranger his whole life, knowing that his community of origin was simultaneously seen as inferior and as a threat.[4] It must have been disorienting to know he was born to an oppressed community but was raised and educated in the heart of the oppressive empire. Moses could have enjoyed the comforts of Egypt, aligning himself with power and prestige, and forgotten his own people. He could have assimilated into this environment, but something in him does not let him do so—his destiny remains inextricably linked to his people, the Hebrews.

Camacho notes the similarities between the Hebrews and Latinx immigrants: "The Pharaoh in Moses' story approached the Hebrew people as dangerous invaders in spite of the fact that they had been there for generations. It didn't matter that they had originally arrived in Egypt as refugees during a famine or had helped build up the kingdom. Similarly, although cheap Latinx labor has been used to build and maintain the United States, Latinx immigrants have become scapegoats for everything that's wrong in society. How or why we ended up here remains an afterthought."[5]

Having the option, Moses chooses the side of the oppressed. Though reluctant at first, he becomes God's chosen leader for delivering the Hebrew people. I have often wondered whether God chose Moses because he was someone who understood both cultures. As a Hebrew who understood the ins and outs of Egypt, he had integrated but not assimilated into Egyptian culture. The difference between Moses's approach and Joseph's is nuanced but distinct. Those who assimilate identify wholly with their host country's culture and deny or suppress their own, but those who integrate learn to navigate the basic values and principles of the society they live in while maintaining their distinctive cultural identities and practices. Essentially, those who integrate live in two worlds. For Moses, this means living in the worlds of the oppressed and the oppressor simultaneously.

Moses can use his intimate knowledge of Egypt to undermine the empire in subversive ways for the common good. He becomes the anti-Joseph who aligns himself with the oppressed for the sake of their and his liberation. Moses's clarity about the evils of his adopted Egyptian culture might be the difference between assimilation and integration. Integration is necessary for immigrants but is *not* destructive to us. In fact, it can serve the common good because often we can see things more objectively in our host cultures when we are not absorbed into them like water to a sponge.

Such is the case of Bennet Omalu, the doctor who exposed the prolonged effect of concussions on NFL players. As a Nigerian immigrant, Dr. Omalu was disinterested in and confused by the North American fascination with football.[6] Although he lived and worked in the US and in a city where football reigns supreme, Dr. Omalu remained outside this American fascination as well as other aspects of American culture. Morbid as it may seem to many North Americans, he saw himself as an "advocate for the dead," a calling he embraced wholeheartedly, as he sought to defend and speak for those who died from traumatic brain injuries.[7] His calling led him to do research and learn from NFL players whose lives had ended tragically and had been forgotten, their football glory days far behind them.

Indeed, he became their champion and defender, standing up to the league and its doctors, who communicated to him, between the lines, "We own this field. We are not going to bow to some no-name Nigerian."[8] But it was the outsider, a foreigner, who exposed the harm inflicted on players who were discarded by society once they were past their prime and no longer productive. He became not only their defender but also the face of their cause. And it was in part he who forced the NFL to admit and reckon with the consequences of a sport where men sustain traumatic head injuries over and over again. Dr. Omalu's integration but not assimilation enabled him to speak truth to power, just as Moses did thousands of years ago.

Good Advocacy

I am no longer a teacher, but I often speak and write about biblical justice and immigration. In this context I often hear people say that immigrants do not assimilate. As a good advocate, I am supposed to say, "Yes, they do!" and prove to them that this is a myth. I am supposed to help mostly white Christians forget that most first-generation immigrants struggle with American culture and the English language and do not assimilate. I am supposed to reassure them instead that immigrants do assimilate, learn English, and lose their own culture and language within a couple of generations. In essence, I am supposed to convince them that immigrants will become white and will not change the North American cultural and religious landscape.[9]

Naturally, most immigrants to North America today will not literally become white; they originate in Asia, Africa, Latin America, and the Middle East. But many North Americans, including those in the church, want reassurance that the mythical melting pot is alive and well—that immigrants will quickly assimilate to the dominant culture, even if they are brown or Black or Asian. What many of those people want is reassurance that the white-dominant culture will remain undisturbed and will continue to be the norm. They want the comfort of knowing that white supremacy will not be toppled, though they would never use those words explicitly.

The message of assimilation makes me uncomfortable because it requires me to celebrate the loss of other people's culture, traditions, and languages in order to alleviate the fears that white people, including Christians, might have about a diverse society where their position as power brokers of society may be threatened. It is akin to saying, "White Christians, please do not fear immigrants because they, too, will submit to white supremacy and blend into it as best as they can, even with their non-white skin and features." I refuse to communicate that message because it is not my job to appease privileged white Christians at the expense of the dignity of immigrants. Nor is it my job to absolve anyone of their Christian responsibility to welcome and love immigrants because they are nostalgic for a bygone era of *Leave It to Beaver*, before the civil rights movement and second-wave feminism.

And I do not want to communicate this message because I know what it is like to live with the self-hatred brought on by internalized racism and beliefs about the cultural superiority of white America, and I recognize the damage that did to my sense of self and the people around me. Assimilation is rooted in white supremacy because it assumes that our white host culture is superior and that we must shake off our inferior cultures to belong. But it does not have to be this way. Centering immigrants in our Christian response to immigration means that we make room for their integration but do not pressure them to assimilate. We recognize that people are allowed to bring their full selves into every space even as they are adapting to a new country. The act of speaking another language, eating the food of one's homeland, and listening to music from our cultures is not a threat to the host country's way of life, because immigrants value integration just as much as the native citizens do.

In truth, I am still recovering from the harm inflicted on me by the pressure to assimilate. I often remember those middle-school students at my first teaching job and wish I had followed their example—they were truly integrating into American culture and life while being true to their whole selves. I wish I could go back and seek their forgiveness for not standing up for them and instead distancing myself from them. My journey toward a healthier sense of self started with them and, sadly, not in the church.

I was told that the church valued diversity—later I discovered that this actually meant that they valued seeing Black and brown faces in the congregation but that they did not welcome Black and brown people as teachers, leaders, and decision-makers. In essence, the church also wanted my assimilation into their way of being. It was acceptable to be brown as long as I talked and behaved like the majority-white congregation and knew my place.

Among Christians of color who actively resist white supremacy and embrace the Jesus who loves and accepts people as they are, I have begun to love my true self. It is those friends and that Jesus who are continually teaching me to affirm that I am not just a child of God but also a Latina immigrant child of God, a Guatemalan-American child of God. Jesus does not ask me or anyone to assimilate but asks us to be fully ourselves.

God of Joseph and Moses,

You gave us a vision of the world that is just, generous, and life-giving for all. You created each of us in your image, whether we were born Egyptians, Hebrews, or North Americans. You are the God of all peoples and cultures, revealing yourself locally and globally so that we may know you. As God in the flesh, you were a fully integrated Jewish man who held on to your heavenly identity. We confess that we are people who tend toward fear of those who look, speak, and act differently than we do. Enable us by your Spirit not to fear differences but to celebrate them. Show us how to live together and give each other space to be who you created us to be. We need your wisdom to reimagine our understanding of what it means to adapt to another country and culture. Help us to see a way forward that does not harm our immigrant neighbors but respects their cultures and languages. Amen.

2

The Scarlet Cord and the Myth of the Good Immigrant

> Matthew lists Rahab as one of the ancestresses of the Lord Jesus Christ, and that may be one reason why there was something about free-wheeling ladies with warm and generous hearts that he was never quite able to resist.
>
> —Frederick Buechner, *Peculiar Treasures*

Joshua is on the cusp of leading the Israelites into the promised land, the land flowing with milk and honey that their parents had dreamed of in the wilderness. The nation is ready to move, ready to fight for the land Yahweh promised them. But first, two spies enter the city to scope things out . . . and they meet a Canaanite prostitute named Rahab.

Rather than follow Joshua's specific instructions ("Go, view the land, especially Jericho"; Josh. 2:1), the spies go straight to the house of Rahab in the city wall, where they spend the night. The text suggests that they may have even received sexual favors from her. Many Christians and other people are deeply uncomfortable with Rahab's profession. Throughout history, preachers, teachers, biblical scholars, and even some of the church fathers have tried to turn her into an affluent innkeeper, since Rahab owns her home and seems to be a woman of independent means. I am sure they simply want a more respectable profession for this woman of God. Understandably, some people prefer not to imagine a foreign prostitute in the lineage of Jesus. Some may even believe that patriarchal retellings of her story have changed Rahab's profession to discredit her, but the text calls her a *zōnâ* ("zonah") in ancient Hebrew, which is best understood as a prostitute.[1] For our purposes, we will use the modern term "sex worker" because it gets to the heart of the economic reasons behind Rahab's work—it was a means of survival. Even her very name, probably a nickname, carries sexual overtones—"Rahab" means "wide" or "broad."[2]

The Israelites' own history with foreign women and God's command to them in Deuteronomy 7 sets us up as readers to expect an entirely different story: "When the Lord your God brings you into the land that you are about to enter and occupy, and he clears away many nations before you—the Hittites, the Girgashites, the Amorites, *the Canaanites*, the Perizzites, the Hivites, and the Jebusites, seven nations mightier and more numerous than you—and when the Lord your God gives them over to you and you defeat them, then *you must utterly destroy them. Make no covenant with them and show them no mercy*" (vv. 1–2).

But as it turns out, Rahab knows everything that Yahweh has done for the Israelites—word of the exodus and their years in the wilderness reached her ears far away in Jericho. Biblical scholar Megan McKenna notes that because Rahab's house is built right into the city wall, she hears all kinds of stories, news, and gossip as people come and go; after all, her house is a place many men pass through, which makes her privy to all kinds of information.[3] And having heard of the greatness of their God, she decides to cast her lot with theirs and chooses not only to hide the spies but to protect them by lying to the king's messengers regarding their whereabouts. Contrary to God's command, the spies swear an oath to this Canaanite woman: she will hide and protect them, and they, in turn, will save her and her family when the Israelites destroy the city of Jericho.

Reading the story, I found Rahab's conversion very convenient. Was she truly a believer, or was she simply trying to survive? Was she motivated by her commitment to this foreign god and the great deeds she has heard about or by her human desire to protect her family and herself? Does she lie to protect the spies and honor a higher call, or is she just a clever trickster?

It is difficult to know her intentions, but whether or not Rahab's conversion was real, she did what she promised to do. The text regards Rahab positively, making no judgment on her lies to the king's messengers. In fact, she is the only person in the story who has agency.[4] Joshua, the king of Jericho, the king's messengers, and even God are depicted as passive in Joshua 2. By contrast, Rahab is a well-rounded character who guides the narrative; it is she who lies to the king's messengers about the whereabouts of the spies, and it is she who tells the spies where to hide—commands they willingly obey.

Biblical scholar Cristina García-Alfonso highlights that Rahab is a financially independent woman who is both an insider and an outsider. She is a Canaanite and, as such, a member of the community. But because she is a sex worker, she is an outsider even among the Canaanites, and she experiences the marginalization that comes with her profession in the ancient world. She is a foreigner in her own land, all the more so given that she lives in the city wall on the periphery of her city, meaning she is literally on the margins.[5] Her status as an insider and an outsider may help us understand why she would so easily betray her own people. García-Alfonso goes on to say, "She had no strong ties to her people, and, feeling excluded from society, Rahab recognized the possibility of survival for herself and her family."[6]

The spies keep their part of the bargain with Rahab, disregarding God's command not to swear oaths with Canaanites and not to show them any mercy (Deut. 7:2). This Canaanite has a face and a name and is clearly not wicked, as God's word had said all Canaanites would be (9:5)—so the spies make an exception for the helpful Rahab, acknowledging that she does not fit the stereotype of the evil Canaanite. It is an exception fraught with ambiguity and contradiction because her profession suggests she is exactly the kind of person the ban should apply to. But she surprises us by confessing faith in Yahweh with clarity and conviction.[7] She says,

> I know that the Lord has given you the land, and that dread of you has fallen on us, and that all the inhabitants of the land melt in fear before you. For we have heard how the Lord dried up the water of the Red Sea before you when you came out of Egypt, and what you did to the two kings of the Amorites that

> were beyond the Jordan, to Sihon and Og, whom you utterly destroyed. As soon as we heard it, our hearts melted, and there was no courage left in any of us because of you. The LORD your God is indeed God in heaven above and on earth below. (Josh. 2:9–11)

Is it possible that, by placing her story at the beginning of the book of Joshua, before the conquest of the land, the text's author invites us to consider who can and cannot belong to the people of Israel? Is her inclusion a reminder that Yahweh always intended to be the God of *all* people? Those whom God's people are inclined to reject remain central to God's purposes, and Rahab will live in Israel with honor, accepted as family. From Matthew 1:5 we learn that Rahab married a man named Salmon from the tribe of Judah and became the great-great-grandmother of King David, Jesus's ancestor.

The conquest of Jericho happens through a wall in the city; the words and actions of a foreign sex worker are the means by which God enters Jericho. Rahab's inclusion as one of Israel's own is so complete that the details of her salvation recall the exodus and the Passover: her house is marked with a sign, a red cord, that will allow death to pass over her entire family, a sign to the Israelites to spare her household from destruction.[8]

It is clear in the story of Rahab that the people of God are not defined by ethnicity or even by moral purity or goodness but by their faith and commitment to the God of Israel.

Bad Immigrants

When I was in eighth grade, my mom never failed to voice her strong disapproval of my best friend, Marilyn. It wasn't that

Marilyn did anything in particular to my mom or to me; my mom just did not like that Marilyn was Puerto Rican. My mom's anecdotal experience suggested that because Puerto Ricans did not have to struggle for legal status, they were content to migrate to the US mainland and live off public benefits. "Is that what you want? To get pregnant and live off the government?" she would ask me.

In retrospect, I recognize that my mom wanted to protect me. I was her oldest child, a daughter, and now that I was a teenager and no longer content to play with dolls and watch cartoons, she worried. She knew of dangers that I could not imagine. However, viewing the world through her own prejudices and limited emotional resources, she did not know how to articulate her concern apart from harmful stereotypes and nagging fearmongering about worst-case scenarios. In her mind, her words said, "I love you, and I want you to be safe." But I did not hear them that way.

To my thirteen-year-old mind, my mom's insistence that I end my friendship with Marilyn made no sense. It seemed unfair to judge my friend based on her place of origin. Marilyn and I talked about makeup, clothes, and boys. We lent each other hair accessories and walked to school together. Marilyn was the first person to attempt to teach this very stiff, rhythmless Latina to dance merengue. We complained about teachers and shared a mutual hatred for pre-algebra. I have no idea if Marilyn's family received public benefits, but I do know that neither of us wanted to have a baby in our teens. For all my mom's worries, Marilyn was no bad influence; we were normal teenagers with normal teenage concerns. I ignored my mom's comments and dismissed them as out of touch.

Nonetheless, my mom's words communicated two important messages that I internalized deeply from this and hundreds of other conversations:

1. Our family had come to the United States to work and improve our lives.
2. It was important to distinguish ourselves from other migrants who we believed did not.

Years later, when I faced a long season of unemployment and severe anxiety and depression, my mom's words haunted me. Though she didn't intend this, her words set in motion a subtle but harmful shift in me—a shift that would be detrimental to my wholeness and well-being for the next few decades.

Since graduating from college, I had never been without gainful employment. I worked as a teacher, then transitioned to the nonprofit world, specializing in human resources and program management. I was a good immigrant who worked, paid her taxes, and contributed to the common good . . . until I wasn't.

Now I had been laid off; I had moved back east to live with my brother and sister-in-law who generously opened up their home in Maryland to me; and I was clinically depressed and without my support system, since I was far from my community in California.

In my long days alone, I never once thought of Rahab, who pleased God so much she became part of God's family. Instead, I thought about the fact that I was exactly the kind of immigrant nobody wanted to include: someone who was not working and who collected unemployment benefits. On top of that, I was not well. I finally came to accept that since middle school I had struggled with moderate to severe depression and anxiety. I had left them untreated, wanting to believe that this was just normal sadness that everyone experiences. But now it had become a disability—I could barely function and had suicidal ideation. What country wants an unemployed, mentally ill immigrant?

With the benefit of hindsight, I see that there is a name for what I felt through that season: shame. Shame and I were well acquainted, close friends even. This friendship prevented me from genuine connection and vulnerability with real people who wanted to know and care for me. When a kind high school teacher asked me what was wrong and why my grades were suddenly faltering, shame kept me from telling her about my parents' crumbling marriage and the ensuing chaos and instability in our home. When college friends were excited to go home for the holidays, shame kept me from telling them that after my mother's death, my dad, in his grief, had descended so deeply into alcoholism that I felt the loss of both my parents, even while one was still physically present. The last thing I wanted to do was go home.

The insidious thread that runs through it all is that I never opened up to tell my story because I aspired to be the good kind of immigrant. I generally pride myself on not caring much what people think, but in my mind my family and I were perpetual guests in the US. I wanted people to think well of us because if they did not, were we really worthy of inclusion and belonging?

I never realized the toll that trying to achieve a "good immigrant" status took on me. Not only did it keep me from living fully into my identity as a child of God who bears the image of God, but it also kept me from seeing my own immigrant family and neighbors through the lens of the gospel. Instead, I demanded this impossible standard from them as well, evaluating them through the same rubric of worthiness that was used to evaluate me. In simple terms, my aspirations for "good immigrant" status drew me *away* from the gospel and Christian community, not *toward* them.

I love the story of Rahab because that cunning woman who lies and makes her living from sex work is exactly the kind of person most people want to exclude from their family or nation. She challenges everything the Israelites believed about goodness, worthiness, and inclusion. Like so many immigrants today, Rahab values survival above all. But unlike many of us, she does not seem to question whether she is worthy of inclusion. She seems to know deep in her soul that her status as a human being is enough to make her deserving of belonging.

The Myth of the Good Immigrant

I do not know any good immigrants.

Good immigrants, according to American mythology, work hard and keep their heads down, never dreaming of accessing public benefits. They are eternally grateful for admission to this great country and never critique it. They speak English fluently, without an accent, and fully assimilate into American culture, forgetting the old country except in the occasional nostalgic moment or holiday. They do the jobs nobody else wants to do, which means they are essential but invisible. They are so law-abiding as to be above reproach. In short, good immigrants are shining examples of what it means to be American.

Above all, good immigrants manage to maintain legal status amid an ever-shifting legal landscape that favors some and marginalizes others, leaving many stranded in a world of loopholes and technicalities, leaving families hungry and in danger, separated and unsure of the future. Some might even go so far as to say that good immigrants would see their children starve before they would cross a border without papers. It's a mythical status of perfection that no one can achieve.

The epitome of the good immigrant mythology are the DREAMers (Development, Relief, and Education for Alien Minors) or DACA (Deferred Action for Childhood Arrivals) recipients in the US. Because these immigrants were brought to the US as children, they are seen as innocent, not having participated in their parents' decision to enter the country unlawfully. As such, they are said to be deserving of a pathway to citizenship. These adults are now college students and professionals who contribute to society with their work; the vast majority of them speak English and have spotless criminal records.

Without a doubt, I support legislation that allows DACA recipients to gain legal permanent residency and future citizenship. My point of contention is the harmful narrative that holds up these particular immigrants as "good" in contrast to "bad" ones who deserve marginalization and deportation, like their parents, for example. It harms *all* immigrants when we adopt narratives that glorify some and criminalize others, pitting us against each other rather than uniting us in the struggle for the inclusion of all. DACA recipients deserve a pathway to citizenship because they are human beings worthy of belonging. Their parents who speak heavily accented English and committed a criminal misdemeanor when they entered the US deserve a pathway to citizenship for the exact same reason.

Even more insidious than the exaltation of DACA recipients is the way the "good immigrant" narrative harms immigrants with physical, mental, or emotional disabilities. If the only good immigrants are those who work hard, then are immigrants with disabilities considered bad immigrants because they cannot work? Are they automatically excluded?

My friend Beth Watkins works with resettled refugees who have medical needs or who are survivors of violence and torture. Some of the people she works with come from countries with active conflicts and have suffered physical disabilities, whether permanent or temporary, as a result. Some are physically able-bodied but live with mental and/or emotional trauma and are in need of mental health care and support. It is a challenge for her to provide them the support they need in a timely manner. For refugees, it is usually easier to access job-seeking services than mental health services. Beth often shares how angry and disillusioned it makes her that in the US the support and social services for refugees seem to be inherently ableist, since they cater to those who are able-bodied and who can lay aside the trauma of displacement in order to work. The message is clear: you were brought here to work.

Immigrants with disabilities are harmed by narratives that suggest only those who work and produce are good and worthy of belonging. As Christians, we should value a society that provides places of safety where healing can take place and not just places where people can work and serve. After all, the defining message of our faith is that we are saved and made whole *not* by our own works but by the grace of our God.

We have to wonder . . . is it biblical or even practical to think of people as good or bad immigrants?

I am not a good immigrant. What I am is an image bearer of God with flaws, struggles, and habitual sins. No more can be asked of me or of any immigrant than you might expect from yourself as a North American. Nothing magical happens in the act of migration that makes one person better than another. In fact, the expectation that immigrants should be better than the average North American is not grounded in historical reality or in the examples we see in the Scriptures.

North American history reveals that the immigrants who arrived in earlier centuries did not migrate to Canada and the US to become good Americans or good Canadians but to replicate the best of their old country in a more favorable environment and under better circumstances.[9] That is why, in the US, we have *New* England in the northeast, Little Italy in several American cities, and Pennsylvania Dutch country. These early immigrants didn't think of themselves as legal or illegal because that language was not part of their vocabulary; they simply moved across our borders with ease, often without so much as an interview, as there was no mechanism to enforce the few immigration laws that existed. Today, many Americans assume that these early immigrants quickly learned English and integrated into American society, but historians have disproven many of these ideas. The uncomfortable truth is that immigrants have not changed—we share the same needs and the same flawed humanity. It is immigration laws and their enforcement that have changed.

American historian Maria Cristina Garcia notes, "During much of our [US] history people moved across our border with ease. If your ship docked outside of New York City, chances were you weren't even interviewed."[10] The Chinese Exclusion Act (1882) was one of the first immigration laws to be instituted, but unless Chinese immigrants were coming through major ports of entry, there was no way to find and refuse them entry to the US.[11] These were the days before the Immigration and Customs Enforcement (ICE) or the border patrol agencies existed—they were not founded until nearly fifty years later.

Even the immigrants described in the Bible struggled with human frailties that are recorded for all of us to read. We can turn to our Bibles and find stories of imperfect immigrants, saints seeking to live as faithfully as they can in a land that is not their own.

Naomi migrates to Moab, escaping a famine and seeking economic security for her family (Ruth 1). Her sons marry Moabite women, which God's law prohibited (Deut. 23:3; Ezra 9:1–3; Neh. 13:1–3). Later, ignoring God's law yet again, Naomi instructs her Moabite daughter-in-law Ruth to pursue and marry Boaz, a man from Bethlehem (Ruth 3:1–4).

Abram, fleeing a different famine, migrates to Egypt and commits fraud by presenting Sarai as his sister instead of as his wife. He then traffics her for his own gain (Gen. 12:10–16). It is God who steps in to rescue Sarai (10:17).

In the New Testament, a Syrophoenician woman, unknown and unrelated to Jesus, invades his privacy to seek a favor (Mark 7:24–30). Most of us miss the scandal in this encounter, but it is an affront to Jesus and his honored status as a Jewish man to have an unclean foreign woman approach him. Unexpectedly, the encounter ends with Jesus granting her the favor and affirming her faith.

All of these flawed biblical heroes, including Rahab, are held up as pillars of the faith, examples for us Christians to follow. We recognize that these imperfect people bore the *imago Dei* and that God's plans and purposes are made known to us through them. God saw them as friends and beloved children and did not allow their offenses to overshadow their identities, nor did God demand perfection before including them in God's kingdom purposes.

Flawed Human Beings

Most countries want laborers, quiet ones who will hopefully return home when their work is done. What they receive are human beings. And these human beings come with the struggles that all humans face. For all my shame at the explosive breakup of my parents' marriage, it is not only immigrants who deal with the brutal and painful end of intimate relationships. For all my shame at my father's alcoholism, it is not just immigrants who struggle with addictions. For all my shame at managing my mental illness, depression and anxiety are not unique to immigrants. These problems are common to human beings, no matter where they come from or where they live.

When I worked in church engagement for immigration advocacy, I would tell the stories of immigrants in the community of Baltimore. I confess that I often told stories of immigrants leading exemplary lives of hard work and quiet perseverance, reinforcing this harmful myth of good immigrants and bad immigrants. But one day I engaged in an experiment. While at an affluent Baltimore church, I told the story of a regular man, an immigrant in the community who might have married a US citizen solely for the purpose of getting permanent US residency. Once he had legal status, he swiftly divorced his American wife. This man worked two jobs: the Amazon warehouse by day and Uber driving by night. He saved money from every paycheck so that he could sponsor an immigrant visa for each one of his children in his Caribbean home country. And he enjoyed smoking marijuana on the side. In fact, he talked very openly about it, even before it was legal. With the help of an immigration attorney, he became a US citizen despite having been arrested for drug possession.

I am not sure if the people in the church were aware, but the more details I shared about this man's life, the more they shook their heads, revealing their disapproval. One of them said aloud, "This is not the kind of immigrant you want to talk about if you want people to care about immigrants!" Indeed, she was correct. And it is precisely why these are not the stories you read about or hear from most immigration advocates who are working within white Christian spaces.

Still, I wonder how many people in that church ever smoked marijuana before it was legal? I wonder how many of them fudged the truth on their taxes to avoid paying their full liability? How many divorced their partners for less than honorable reasons? How many sped on the highway and rolled through stop signs? How many had lied to police officers to talk their way out of a traffic citation? These neighbors would have denied Rahab inclusion in their Baltimore community. I am sure they believe themselves worthy of understanding and second chances, but they could not extend that grace to immigrants in their community.

The white church at large also fails to extend that grace to immigrants in North America and Europe. And when they do so, they deny our very humanity, our own *imago Dei*, because they expect more from us immigrants even than from our own Lord Jesus Christ. The Gospels recount stories from the life of Jesus where his full humanity is on display: he is at times tired (John 4), frustrated with religious leaders (Mark 3), grieved and saddened (John 11), and angered to the point of turning over tables in the temple (Matt. 21). He takes breaks from his disciples to be alone with his father (Mark 1), and he naps in a boat while the disciples tremble in fear (Luke 8).

Jesus's own humanity was complex and multifaceted. His history included both forced migration as a child refugee and persecution under a foreign empire. His incarnation invites us all to be courageous enough to fully and unreservedly embrace our own and each other's humanity. In our shared life in Christ, we do not escape our humanity or take it from one another but rather delve more deeply into it, choosing to love our neighbors as ourselves, even our imperfect immigrant neighbors.

Subscribing to the rhetoric of the good and bad immigrant leads Western Christians away from recognizing the *imago Dei* in their immigrant neighbors and reduces them to arms that work for them rather than human beings that bear God's image, their siblings. And when the *imago Dei* is marred in one of us, it is marred in all of us. God sees us all as beloved children and friends. Do we see as God sees? What needs to change in us so that we see our neighbors as God sees them? How can the church empower immigrants to walk the earth like Rahab did, knowing we have every right to be wherever we have made our home?

God of Rahab,

We are grateful that you don't expect perfection from us before including us in your family. You are the God of all people, regardless of how society views them. The people society rejects are central to your purposes in the world—the ones we dishonor live with honor among your people, just as Rahab did. Conform our Christian communities to your ways of seeing, to your ways of inclusion. We want to love and see as you do. We don't want to be content with the ways things are, with parsing out good and bad immigrants, worthy and unworthy people. Be near to immigrants who feel the pressure of this rubric of worthiness and liberate them from its unfair and dehumanizing expectations. Lead immigrants as you led Rahab to see and know her worth as a human being. Immigrants need not be dignified because you have already dignified them—they need only remember their worth as your children. Help them to know it. Liberate all of us from narratives that rob us and our neighbors of our humanity. Amen.

3 Russian for Beginners

Words Matter

> Language shapes the way we think and determines what we can think about.
>
> —Benjamin Lee Whorf, *Language, Thought, and Reality*

I stood at the airline ticket counter in the Boston airport, eager to board my flight back to Kazakhstan. The former Soviet state had been my home for the past year, but I had been back in the United States to celebrate my sister's wedding. I waited anxiously, worried I would not be able to fall asleep on the flights and would arrive bleary-eyed and exhausted; I simultaneously worried I *would* sleep and would wake up drowsy and incoherent. My uneasy thoughts were occasionally disrupted by the recognition of a Russian word or two spoken in the line behind me. Apparently, I was not the only one headed to the former Soviet Union.

My backpack accidentally bumped the young woman waiting with her companions behind me, and I instinctively said, "Izvineetye, pazhalusta." ("Excuse me, please" in Russian.) They all looked at me in surprise—then their faces relaxed into broad, relieved smiles. After our brief exchange in Russian, where I explained how I happened to know a bit of the language, they asked if I would be willing to walk their elderly, non-English-speaking babushka (grandmother) through security and to the gate since we were on the same flight. I promised I would, and we chatted all the way to the entrance of the security line, where I watched them engage in the forlorn rituals of goodbye: hugs, kisses, tears, words of love, and promises to call and write and, most of all, not to forget.

They thanked me. Their babushka smiled at me, released their hands, and grabbed on to my hand as if we had made an exchange and she now belonged with me. She and I walked through security and all the way to our gate. We sat down, and she told me her name was Lyubov (the Russian word for "love") or Lyuba for short, that she was an ethnic Russian Jew from a village in northern Kazakhstan. Most of her friends had moved to Israel, so her granddaughters wanted her to stay in America with them. But she could not adjust to life here; she thought learning English would be too difficult. Lyuba dug through her multiple plastic bags until she found some cookies she wanted to share with me, and I bought us both hot tea while the time passed.

She spoke Russian much faster than most people I talked to did. She clearly did not speak to many beginners like me, but thankfully, I knew enough to catch the gist of the conversation, even if not every word. Before the flight, I asked the attendant at the boarding desk if it was possible for us to sit together, so I could remain in the company of my new traveling companion. He was happy to oblige.

After almost twenty-four hours of travel, I said goodbye to Babushka Lyuba at the baggage claim in the Astana airport, where she took my face in both her hands with a gleeful "Spasibo bolshoe!" (Thank you very much!)

This is *not* a story that ends in a lasting friendship or in finding a grandmother-figure of my own while I lived abroad. I never saw Babushka Lyuba again. But looking back on that experience, I wonder how things might have turned out differently had I bumped into her granddaughter and said "Excuse me" in English instead of in Russian.

I was in the United States and had every right to speak in English with the expectation of being understood; yet somehow hearing the Russian speakers behind me prompted me to speak their language. Those simple words in a language I barely knew opened the door to a conversation and a traveling companion. Those simple words were the pathway to trust that encouraged the young women to commend their beloved grandmother to my temporary care. Those simple words opened the circle of their affection and ushered me inside, even if temporarily. This was not the most important encounter of my life, but I marvel at the grace of it: the distraction from my anxiety and the warmth and contentment I felt in our time together after feeling lost and wistful all summer long. As much as we might boast of our independence, we human beings clearly impact one another: the actions we take, the words we speak, and the feelings we show influence those around us and reveal how deeply we need each other.

I was not fluent in Russian. I would have been more comfortable speaking in English—but then Babushka Lyuba could not have communicated with me. It would have been impossible for her. My uncomfortable struggle to communicate allowed me to be a friend to her in a time of need. And to her it mattered tremendously that I chose to communicate in *her* heart language, even if it was difficult for me, even though my grammar was not perfect.

Over the years I've seen how effective choosing our own discomfort can be in crossing cultures and building bridges of understanding. My friend Marisa—a blonde, blue-eyed American—grew up in the Philippines and speaks Tagalog like a native. When Filipino immigrants visited our workplace, she spoke to them in Tagalog, and their faces lit up. They would not have to use the translator they had brought along, and they were charmed by their conversation with her, as if they all shared a secret. Similarly, my friend Andrea spent a few years teaching English in South Korea. When we visited a restaurant in Koreatown in Los Angeles, she spoke to the servers in Korean—much to their surprise and delight. It was clear that they did not often encounter people who looked like her but spoke *their* language.

The ethos of a room changes when we meet people on their terms and not ours—when we use their language and not our own—when we give up our comfort for the sake of theirs. Words, it is very clear, have power and can open doors. And this remains true even when we only speak one language. The words we speak within our own language can turn others into outcasts and perpetual outsiders; our words have the power not just to disparage but also to dehumanize others, even leading to violence against them. Alternatively, the words we speak can be life-giving and empowering to others; these words can alter how we see and, therefore, how we act in specific social situations, encouraging equity and justice in our encounters.

We need look no further to understand the power of words than the Gospel of John, where Jesus himself is described as a word.

As a lover of language, I have always been fascinated by the description of Jesus as a word. When I was a young Christian, the whole concept seemed curious and a bit confusing—the idea that a feathery light word could become flesh seemed incomprehensible. How could that be?

In the prologue to the Gospel of John, the writer says that the Word was in the beginning and became flesh and dwelt among us (1:1–14). "Jesus is the incarnation of God's own Word, the embodiment of God's glory, truth and will, and the way to life with God," says Dr. Marianne Meye Thompson.[1] Many of us were taught that the Bible itself is the Word of God, but John's Gospel opens with a clarion declaration: *Jesus* is the Word of God, and his arrival in the world is no afterthought; Jesus was present with God from the beginning of creation. In Greek, Jesus would have been called the *logos* of God.[2] *Logos* is defined not only as the outward expression of thoughts in speech but also as inward thoughts. And for the Stoic philosophers of John's day, the *logos* was the rational principle that caused the natural creation to grow.[3]

Words as Sticks and Stones

I remember an elementary school teacher training all of us to say, "Sticks and stones may break my bones, but words will never hurt me." She was, I am sure, overwhelmed by tattling little kids complaining of name-calling and wanted to give us an easy way to respond that would leave her out of it. And "sticks and stones" might have helped when someone called you a "ball hog" during recess or said the lunch packed by your immigrant mom smelled yucky. Those words were airy, light, and easy to cast away.

Overall, I found "sticks and stones" to be . . . unsatisfactory. It did not soothe my injured soul when a classmate said I had "icky brown skin" or make me feel better when another said, "Go back to your country!" These words were powerful; I did not recover from them easily. Sometimes I still feel their weight and sting. They reminded me that I am "the other"—a perpetual outsider.

Looking back on those events, I recognize that had I been more aware, it would have been easy to understand that words had power: those words spoken to me in childhood lingered and wounded my own heart for years.

There are so many terrible words in our world, and they shape our realities.

The Uruguayan writer Eduardo Galeano recognizes this truth in his poem "The Nobodies." He describes the way Spanish conquistadors and colonizers used carefully chosen words to dehumanize and devalue the indigenous peoples of the Americas, the nobodies . . .

> *Who don't speak languages, but dialects.*
> *Who don't have religions, but superstitions.*[4]

The colonial settlers understood that it is much easier to enslave and kill those whom you do not recognize as human; it was no challenge to extinguish a subhuman life. Lesser peoples are unworthy of attention and human compassion. It is acceptable to place walls and barriers between us and them, to keep them and their subhuman lives out of ours, to exterminate them if we deem it necessary for our own protection.

Sadly, this seemed to be the understanding of the terrorist responsible for the shooting in El Paso in August 2019 that took the lives of twenty-three people and injured twenty-three others. The shooter said he feared the "Hispanic invasion" of Texas, reflecting the racist language used by former US president Trump, who baselessly used the word "invasion" to describe the humanitarian crisis at the US-Mexico border at least two dozen times.[5] Rather than seeing the humanity he shares with Mexican-Americans and other Latinx people, many of whom are brown skinned, the shooter saw an invasion, a threat to himself and the survival of his own.

Words have power, and there is little doubt in my mind that the former president's xenophobic language influenced this man; violent rhetoric has violent consequences. Former president Donald Trump referred to immigrants and other people as animals, rapists, and criminals and has characterized us as "an infestation."[6] When I think of an infestation, I think of vermin, disgusting creatures like lice, cockroaches, bed bugs, and rats—creatures that are nonhuman, creatures no one cares about when they die, creatures we *want* to die. Applying that horrifying language to human beings all but ensures our rejection of them, our feeling threatened by them, and our seeking to annihilate them. That is the terrible way that words can have destructive power.

Refugee versus Immigrant

Words can cause harm in more subtle ways too. In the fall of 2019, I spoke at a conference in Toronto facilitated by a network of North American Christians who share a common desire to see the church care for those who have been forcibly displaced. Over dinner one night, a few of us Americans and our Canadian hosts discussed the plight of undocumented and economic immigrants in the United States. Bewildered, one of our Canadian friends asked, "Sorry, but can you explain what an 'undocumented' immigrant is? And an 'economic' immigrant?"

We explained some of the most prevalent categories for immigrants in need that the United States identifies: asylee, asylum seeker, undocumented immigrant, economic immigrant, immigrant under temporary protected status, DACA recipient, and refugee. Our hosts nodded their understanding, and one replied flatly, "In Canada, we only have refugees and refugee claimants. Most often, we call them newcomers." The conversation moved on.

I have often thought back to that exchange. All the headlines in the US discuss immigrants and the immigrant crisis at the southern borderlands. Refugees flee a place because their lives are at risk. The legal definition of a refugee person is one who flees their country due to persecution or a well-founded fear of persecution due to their race, nationality, religion, political opinion, or membership in a particular social group.[7] Refugees are literally running from persecution, violence, or the threat of death. It matters very much whether we call people "immigrants" or "refugees," whether we think they are coming because they might have a better life here in North America or because it is the only way they will have *any* life at all. Canadians do not make all the distinctions we do. Their words acknowledge the desperate need of their neighbors and their responsibility to care for them.

Here in the US we prefer to differentiate. You can with a clean conscience tell an immigrant, particularly an economic immigrant who just wants better opportunities for work or education, to go away: "Sorry, go find a better life in some other place." But when you tell a refugee to go away, you are sending them to an almost certain death. In 1939, before World War II, a ship called the *St. Louis* left Europe loaded with Jewish refugees, and they were turned away by the United States, Canada, and Cuba.[8] The refugees on board were forced to return to France, since they found no port that would welcome them. Two-hundred fifty-four of the passengers on board died in concentration camps, approximately half of those who had sought refuge in the Americas. Many more of them suffered internment in the camps but survived.

This is what happens when you tell refugees to go away: they suffer, and they die.

We don't like thinking about that, so we change our language, calling these same people "immigrants" or, worse yet, "illegals"—nameless, faceless immigrants without the legal right to be in the United States. Never mind that "illegal" is an adjective and not a noun—it allows us to reduce a human being to their legal status, thereby absolving ourselves of all responsibility for our neighbors in need. We prioritize processes, laws, and the words that keep us from seeing ourselves in our neighbors, because then we can do what we want but still live with ourselves. Our language has the power to remove humanity; when we reduce a person to a single characteristic of their experience, like legal status or even whether or not they are immigrants, we take away from the image of God in them. For this reason, my friend Sandy Ovalle Martínez always says "refugee person" or "immigrant person." Though she knows it is redundant, she says it reminds her that these are multifaceted and complex human beings in front of her, who are more than their status or their experience of migration.

When I bring up the subject of words and the clear difference in connotation and meaning between a migrant and a refugee, someone will often ask if perhaps I am making too much of words. Perhaps this is not so serious. After all, these are just words—not words that dehumanize or incite violence. Is it possible that these tiny, seemingly insignificant choices do not matter? We all know what we mean, so aren't the specific words we use irrelevant?

Writer and immigrant Phuc Tran addresses this dilemma in his memoir, *Sigh, Gone*: "Do we want words to be powerful or powerless? We can't have it both ways. If we want them to be powerful, we have to act and speak accordingly, handling our words with the fastidious faith that they can do immeasurable good or irreparable harm. But if we want to say whatever we want—if we want to loose whatever words fly into our minds—then we render words powerless, ineffectual, and meaningless."[9] If words have power, if they can shape our realities, then we must be careful how we handle them. After all, the Word took on flesh! The Word that is Jesus came to dwell among us (John 1:14). If we long for words like "justice," "equality," "peace," and "harmony" to take on flesh in our world, then we must be cautious with *all* words, not just the ones that are clearly harmful. Indeed, if we are Jesus's representatives on earth, representatives of the Word, then these beautiful words can take on flesh through us. Those of us who carry his name have chosen to take on the responsibility of taking great care with our words and actions.

In church circles, I frequently hear words about refugees and other immigrants that are meant to be positive, to signify solidarity, care, and concern. These include phrases like "welcome the stranger," "we welcome refugees," "stand with the vulnerable," "be a voice for the voiceless," "we're glad you're our neighbor," and "care for the least of these." While I appreciate the heart and intention of these words, I often wonder about their impact. The dominant church culture's best efforts continue to highlight their own kindness and openness to "the other"—they still center their own posture.

Grammatically speaking, immigrants and refugees are the objects in the above phrases, not the subjects; in other words, we receive the action of those belonging to the dominant church culture but we do not take action ourselves. Very subtly, these words remove humanity from people because they reduce us immigrants to a single characteristic of our experience. While seeming positive, these words have the insidious effect of widening the distance between all of us, between immigrants and the dominant church culture: the more these words become part of everyday vocabulary in the church, the more they inform the imaginations of the dominant church culture and take away from the complex image bearers of God who stand before them.

It is noteworthy that in Matthew 25 Jesus does not command his followers to be kind to those in need. In a complete reversal of expectations, Jesus takes on the very identities of those most marginalized in the ancient world of the first century: "For *I* was hungry and you gave *me* food, *I* was thirsty and you gave *me* something to drink, *I* was a stranger and you welcomed *me*, *I* was naked and you gave *me* clothing, *I* was sick and you took care of *me*, *I* was in prison and you visited *me*" (Matt. 25:35–36). Jesus quite literally sees himself in the poorest and most forgotten people of his time. They are not objects of his charity or hospitality—they are *him*! He commends those who care for him vicariously through the care of others, because the Jesus they worship is the same Jesus they care for in their neighbors in need.[10]

Biblical scholar Anna Case-Winters says, "We need not worry about the timing of the 'second coming.' Christ is already in our midst now and comes to us again and again—unexpectedly—in the form of the person in need. Our response to 'the least of these' is our response to the judge of all the nations."[11] I wonder how advocacy and activism of the dominant church culture might be transformed if they saw themselves in those who live on the margins of society. Rather than flinging a coin to a person experiencing homelessness on the street, they would see their very selves in the need of this neighbor without a home. Rather than feeling pity at media images of refugees in a camp, they would see their own families in the plight of displaced people. Rather than visiting people in immigration detention or prison out of a sense of duty, they would feel their own isolation in the loneliness of their incarcerated neighbors. How would this change their language? Their sense of social responsibility? Their awareness that *they are* their neighbor in need?

Jesus's words and ministry were not disconnected from those whose backs were against the wall. If the North American church seeks to be like him, they need a deeper connection to their neighbors, and that connection must be reflected in their words. I imagine those well-meaning slogans transformed to phrases like "neighbors welcoming neighbors," "all are welcome as we have been welcomed," and "the land that God has shared freely with me, I share freely with you."

Learning and Unlearning

The strangest thing happened to me in Kazakhstan—strange to me but quite common from what I heard from every other aspiring second-language learner: once I knew enough Russian to get around well on my own, I lost my motivation to study and learn more. In Spanish, I would have said, "Me defiendo." I can defend myself; I can survive; I can get what I need; I am competent enough, so why exert more effort when there are so many other things I can do with my time?

It's a rhetorical question but one that deserves an answer because it matters. Because the time spent learning more vocabulary or the proper use of prepositions or the past tense of verbs ultimately would have made me more fluent, more able not just to survive but also to integrate well into the community. "Me defiendo" fluency will never help me understand the nuances of the language, the puns, jokes, and idioms I longed to use so I could speak and understand like a true insider. In fact, during my conversation with Lyuba at the airport and on the plane, all I could think about was how I should have devoted more time to practicing my Russian.

Similarly, learning to use words in ways that honor and humanize immigrants and other people on the margins matters. The effort and time exerted to use inclusive language is not political correctness or a liberal agenda; it is simply respectful and dignifying.

As I have grown in my awareness of how deeply words matter, I know it is important not to refer to God as "he" because God is not male—all of humankind is made in God's image. I have learned to say "enslaved people" instead of "slaves," prioritizing their humanity; and to say "neighbors or siblings" instead of "brothers and sisters," because gender is not limited to two possibilities. I recognize how changing my words has the power to reveal grace and truth, just as it has the power to harm or destroy.

Still, there are so many words to unlearn, to divest of flesh and of their destructive power.

The beauty of this process is that while we unlearn the old words, we learn new words and re-create the world around us. There is no vacuum because the Gospel writer says that the Word was not just born but *dwelled* among us (John 1:14). Jesus, after all, was that Word made flesh that came to live with us. It is our duty as his followers to continue to embody grace and truth in our words, just as he did.

I think of so many words that I want not just to speak but to dwell, make a home, in all our hearts—words that have the power to transform, to speak life, freedom, and inclusion. Words that are core tenets of the gospel. They are words like "love," "justice," "forgiveness," "mercy," and "truth." These words carry light and honor the God we follow. John's Gospel says, "What has come into being in him was life, and the life was the light of all people" (1:3–4).

God of words,

We know our words have limits, but we want our words to mirror yours—we want them to create a better world, to bring beauty and life, to build up and encourage. Keep us from using our words to do harm, even unintended harm. Help us to examine and weigh them knowing that they matter. Let all of our words be seasoned with grace and truth, just as Jesus's words were. Liberate us from the words that separate and unintentionally create a chasm between us. We confess that we grow weary of measuring and thinking through all our words—we are defensive of the words we want to use. Show us how to practice humility in our speech, how to regard others as worthy of care and consideration with the words we use. Give us the imagination to think of new words and expressions, ones that will dignify and be life-giving to all. Amen.

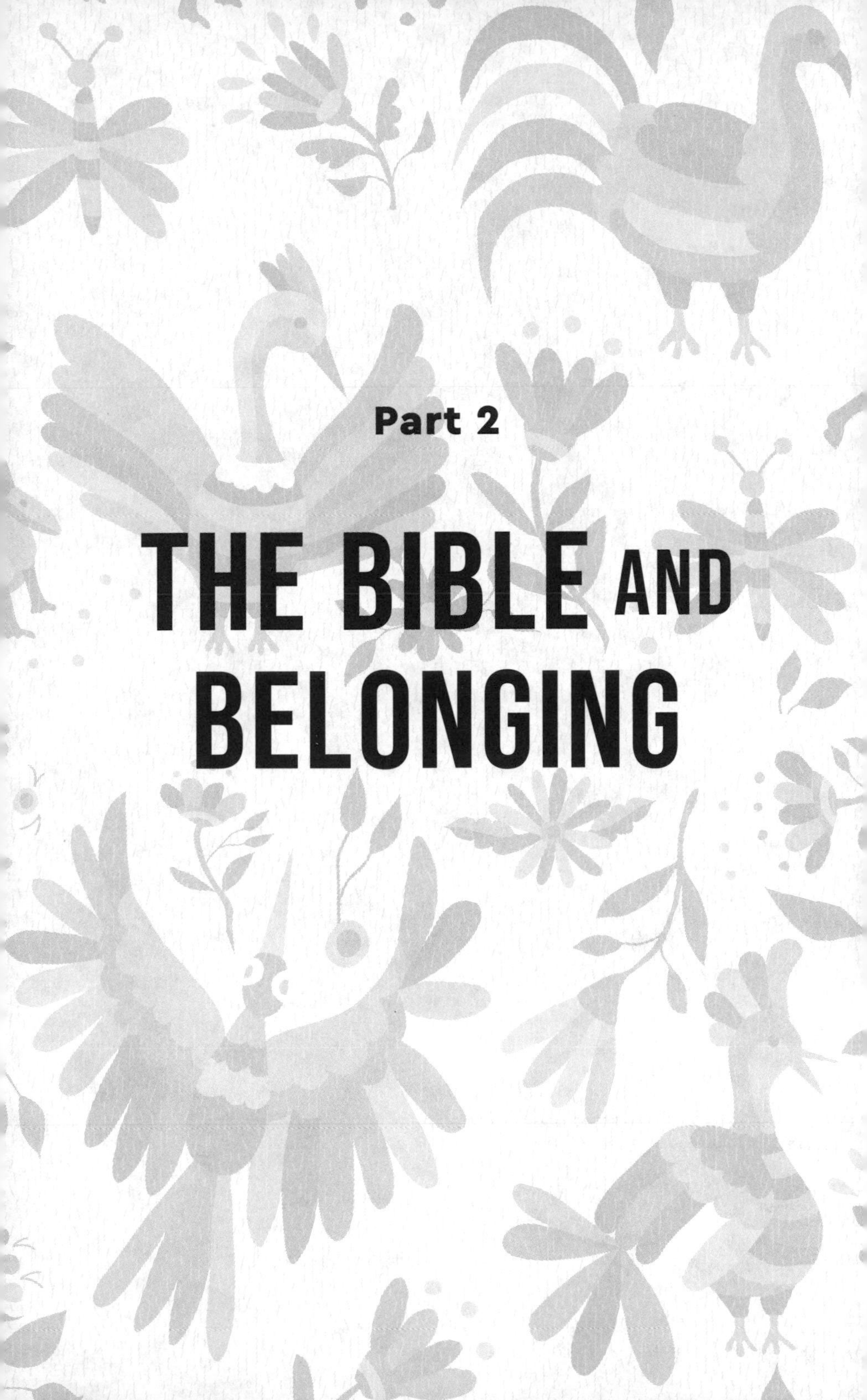

Part 2

THE BIBLE AND BELONGING

4

Reading the Bible

Interpretations Have Consequences

We don't see things as they are. We see things as we are.

—Anaïs Nin, *Seduction of the Minotaur*

So, what stands out to you about this story?" I asked, certain of the answer I would get.

The group of Russian and Kazakh college students in my living room looked at me with blank expressions. We had just finished reading the parable of the prodigal son in Luke 15. Every Friday night, two American teachers and I hosted an investigative Bible study that was mostly tea, cookies, and conversation. Every gathering started with reading and discussing a Bible story.

I was pleased with tonight's choice; it is an easy parable to interpret, after all. Who would not clearly see the father's unconditional love for a son who asked for his inheritance and left town to squander it? But the room fell silent. If there had been a clock, we could have heard its loud, incessant ticking, as our students fidgeted around uncomfortably.

Finally, one student broke the silence: "A . . . famine," he said with hesitation.

The rest of the students nodded. Now it was *our* turn to have blank faces. My American friends and I glanced at each other, trying not to look as bewildered as we felt. But our perceptive students noted our confusion, and one of them said, "During the Great Patriotic War, the fascists surrounded Leningrad. They would not let any food come in, and nobody could go out. Everybody suffered. Many people died. It didn't matter if you were good people or bad people—everyone suffered and died."

I didn't even remember a famine being mentioned in the story. But there it was, printed clearly on my sheet of paper in black and white: "When he had spent everything, *a severe famine* took place throughout that country, and he began to be in need" (Luke 15:14).

I wish I could say that I respectfully listened and sought to understand their perspective. Instead, I panicked. What had we done wrong? This parable was supposed to be an easy way to talk about God's love, our own fallenness as sinners who squander God's gifts, and a return to a heavenly Father who forgives and loves generously. Hours earlier I had imagined this evening much differently: there would be a kind of altar call where students would come forward, and the night would end with saved souls finally awake to a merciful and loving God. I had even imagined writing my newsletter late into the night and telling my home church about the way the Scriptures had come alive and moved the hearts of my students to follow Jesus.

Truth be told, I do not even remember how the evening ended. But the next morning, I lay in bed mulling over the night's events, trying to figure out what had gone so wrong. Where had we turned left instead of right? Did we zig instead of zag? Where had we led our students away from the one and only correct reading of this story?

Sometime later, I came across this verse that quotes Jesus himself: "But I say to you, Love your enemies and pray for those who persecute you, so that you may be children of your Father in heaven; *for he makes his sun rise on the evil and on the good, and sends rain on the righteous and on the unrighteous*" (Matt. 5:44–45). That is exactly what our students had seen in the parable—the difficult and unsettling truth that under certain conditions, like a famine, everyone suffers, and that under others, like rainfall for the crops, everyone prospers, regardless of what kind of people they are. Could it be that they were right? That this was a truth communicated in the parable that I simply did not see?

I could not conceive of it, but I also could not let it go. Their interpretation would certainly be consistent with what New Testament scholars have concluded: parables are supposed to be uncomfortable and provocative to the listener or reader.[1]

Looking back on my time in the former Soviet Union, I understand why the famine mentioned in the parable evoked the powerful memory of Leningrad and another famine. World War II, known in that part of the world as the Great Patriotic War, is a big part of the collective memory of people in the former Soviet Union, even for those who were not alive during Soviet times. Nearly every family experienced loss during the war; an estimated twenty-seven million Soviet citizens lost their lives as a result. Every city, town, and village that I visited had a monument, often with an eternal flame, commemorating this war as well as the courage of those who fought the fascists. All the World War II veterans wore their medals on their clothing for all the world to see and were given free access to public transportation, museums, and other places. May 9 is celebrated as Victory Day, a national holiday to remember the day the war ended and the victory of the Soviet army—it's a day off school and work where you can watch parades in the street and hear stirring speeches on television. World War II is deeply personal to many people in the former Soviet Union, perhaps the way September 11 is personal to many Americans.

When I returned from my time overseas, I told my friend Megan Gearhart about the experience of reading the parable of the prodigal son with my students. It turned out she knew someone who had her own strange experience reading this story with college students in Ethiopia. Her friend had asked her students a question similar to the one I had asked mine: "What stood out to you in the parable?"

They had responded, "He shouldn't have left his family. Why would you leave your family and go somewhere to be alone? Of course things didn't go well for him—he went to a distant country alone!" Megan's friend had been equally baffled by their response. Why didn't the father's love stand out to them? Going to live alone seems a small detail in comparison to a father who loves and forgives no matter what.

I know next to nothing about Ethiopian culture, but I do know that what those students saw in the parable is a truth I have also seen in the Scriptures. In fact, I had been to my friend Annette's wedding where these words had been read: "Two are better than one, because they have a good reward for their toil. For if they fall, one will lift up the other; but *woe to one who is alone and falls and does not have another to help*" (Eccles. 4:9–10).

I could not understand why these students, both mine and the ones in Ethiopia, had missed the point of this parable entirely. Megan and I concluded that the parable of the prodigal son simply did not translate well into all cultures, but I could not shake my discomfort at that conclusion. I felt troubled and confused. This parable communicated what to me was the basic message of the gospel: sinners saved by the grace of a merciful God. If that message did not come through in Central Asia or the Horn of Africa, was it real *anywhere*? Is this core tenet of the gospel seen only with Western eyes? Isn't the gospel universal?

Reading the Bible with my Russian and Kazakh college students—people whose points of view had not been shaped by the Enlightenment and the Western church—created an unresolved tension within me that was the beginning of a spiritual crisis of sorts.

Missing Voices

When I moved to California to attend seminary, I decided to move only the things that fit in my old sedan. This decision translated into having to choose the books I would take with me wisely. As I took inventory and reviewed them, I noticed something I had never noticed before: most of the books that had shaped my faith and formed me spiritually were written by men: John Piper, Jerry Bridges, Richard Foster, Dallas Willard, Eugene Peterson, Bill Hybels, and others. I paused, sitting with the books splayed on the floor, and reflected on all the Bible teachers, mentors, and pastors I had had over the years. Even though I am a woman, an immigrant, and a Latina, my faith had been informed mostly by white people, and not just white people but white men, in particular. Beyond books about Proverbs 31 womanhood and dating relationships, not even a single woman, white or otherwise, had spoken significantly into my life of faith.

Normally, this situation might not have troubled me. I had always reasoned that the only identity that mattered was that I was a Christian. But having spent years living outside the US and reading the Bible with people from another country and culture had not just created tension for me; it had also changed me. My Russian and Kazakh friends read and understood the Bible differently but not incorrectly, as I had first concluded. So, finding my bookshelf filled with the works of white male authors was deeply unsettling.

It isn't that white men do not have a valuable perspective on the Scriptures, because they do. They are made in God's image, too, and God's Spirit had most certainly spoken to others and to me through them. But how could it be that people who looked nothing like me were the only ones shaping my life of faith? If God's church is not just limited to white men, isn't this perspective, at the very least, incomplete? And if my students' cultural perspective was missing from biblical interpretation, what other voices were missing?

These distressing questions led me to an important truth that had begun to settle deep into my bones: we all read the Bible from our social location because we come to the Bible with varied backgrounds, diverse perspectives, and distinct experiences; there's no such thing as *one* correct reading or interpretation of the Bible. My friend Sandy Ovalle Martínez once told me that when she refers to the writing of John Calvin, she calls it French theology, and when she discusses Karl Barth she calls it Swiss theology. She explained that she engages in this naming exercise to remind herself that all theology has a context and comes from a particular perspective.

An Ethnocentric Faith

When I was preparing to live abroad, someone told me that all human beings are ethnocentric—that is, at a subconscious level, or sometimes even consciously, all of us believe that our way of life is the correct way to live, and thus we view other cultures through the lens of our own. This is inevitable, because culture functions much like the Tower of London has: it is both a castle, a place we feel most at home and comfortable, and a prison, a place we cannot see our way out of. "We become certain that our way of doing things is the proper way, and we are blinded to the possibilities of doing things differently. . . . The comfort of our community becomes a bias towards others."[2] The goal, then, is to admit and accept our ethnocentrism and try to become *recovering* ethnocentric people.

For many Christians, the challenging part of becoming recovering ethnocentric people is that most of us do not realize that our expression of faith also carries a culture. We readily admit that being born and raised in the US or Kenya or Nicaragua has not prepared us to live in other contexts. We recognize that we will need to learn a new culture and, perhaps, a new language in a new land. However, we seldom realize that we must also learn a new way of seeing faith in other contexts. When we do not pay attention to how God has been present in another culture and how the Spirit is revealing God's very self in local cultural expressions, we will then impose our own Christian culture on others.

I was guilty of imposing American Christian culture on my Russian and Kazakh friends. I expected them to read the Bible like I did and see the same things I did within its pages. I expected their conversions and discipleship journeys to look like the ones I had seen in the US. I expected my Russian friends to reject the Russian Orthodox Church just as I had rejected the Roman Catholic Church of my upbringing in favor of a more evangelical tradition. None of this was done maliciously or even consciously, though it still did a great deal of harm because we diminished and discounted our friends' experiences of God when they did not look like ours or did not say what we believed were the "right" things. We expected our friends to conform to a white, American, evangelical faith expression because that was the faith we brought, even though they were Kazakhs, Koreans, Tatars, and Russians. God had been with them from the beginning, revealing Godself in ways that are unique to their cultures. These unconscious expectations were reinforced by everything around me: the foreign church plants; the attitudes of the missionaries I knew; the worship songs, whose lyrics had been translated from English; and the hopes and expectations of supporters back home.

Afro-Caribbean scholar Frantz Fanon describes this phenomenon with incisive clarity as he writes about the faith that French colonizers and missionaries brought to Algeria and Haiti: "The church in the colonies is the white people's Church, the foreigner's Church. She does not call the native to God's ways but to the ways of the white man, of the master, or the oppressor."[3]

There is perhaps no better recent example of Christians' lack of awareness about their ethnocentric faith transmission than American author and pastor John MacArthur's assertion that Latin American people do not know Christ. In a video lecture from the Por Su Causa Conference in 2016, MacArthur says, "We all understand that people in the Hispanic world know about Jesus Christ, they know about the Bible, they know about God, they know about salvation, at least in some ways, . . . but they don't know Christ. And they don't know the gospel of grace, and they don't know the full revelation of Scripture."[4] Discounting the very real presence of the Roman Catholic Church since the conquistadors arrived in the Americas in the 1500s, as well as the exponential growth of the Pentecostal Church throughout the region, MacArthur seems to be saying that he does not believe Latin Americans are Christians because their faith expression doesn't look like his.

While MacArthur's views are uncommon, they do reveal an uncomfortable and pervasive truth: many of us believe that the way we live out and practice our faith is the only correct way. It is not difficult to see why many people found MacArthur's comments offensive and racist. What is more difficult to see is how an ethnocentric faith can be dangerous. When Southern Baptist leader Paige Patterson returned to the pulpit after being fired as president of a seminary for making misogynistic comments and mishandling sexual abuse allegations, he preached on the story of Joseph and Potiphar's wife in Genesis.

Joseph is a Jewish patriarch who was falsely accused by an Egyptian woman of sexual assault. Addressing the #MeToo movement, Patterson says, "I have nothing good to say about a woman who falsely accuses a man. She runs the risk of ruining a life. She runs the risk of causing sorrow unknown when the person is, in fact, innocent."[5] He seems to believe that many women lie about sexual harassment and assault (when in fact, statistically, the vast majority of women are telling the truth), and he also implies that his own situation is similar to Joseph's. But is that comparison fair?

Joseph was a vulnerable teenage foreigner in Egypt. He had no power, no friends, and no influence. In fact, Genesis says over and over that only God was with Joseph. Joseph had been trafficked by his brothers and was an enslaved person in the home of Potiphar, the captain of Pharaoh's guard. It was in this state that his enslaver's wife sought to seduce him and then falsely accused him when he refused her advances. Potiphar had him thrown into prison for this false accusation.

In contrast, Patterson is an educated adult white man with a lot of social and institutional power. He was given a pulpit even after a very public employment termination for misogynistic comments he made on the record and for his failure to protect vulnerable people by mishandling abuse allegations. He had many defenders along the way. Rather than being thrown in jail after his accusers came forward, he simply left his job and moved on to other teaching opportunities. In some circles, not even his reputation has suffered.

Patterson and Joseph have so little in common that one wonders why the two would ever be mentioned in the same sentence. Patterson might see himself as Joseph, but were he to read his Bible from the perspective of his accusers, he would see that if he is anyone in Joseph's story, it is Potiphar—the one who refused to listen to Joseph and had him thrown in prison. He is the one who did great harm to people in vulnerable situations, not the one who suffered harm.

Like Patterson, many of us read the Bible from an ethnocentric perspective. We make ourselves the heroes and underdogs of the story rather than understanding our true location in the text. And so we see ourselves as Moses and not Pharaoh, as Mary Magdalene and not Pontius Pilate, as the persecuted first-century church and not the Roman Empire, as Esther and not Haman. Patterson saw himself as Joseph, the victim of injustice, and thus did not see the real victims: those who had suffered sexual abuse and those who were harmed by misogyny. His theological conclusions are dangerous because not only do they *not* lead to seeing rightly and repenting, but they also do great harm to God's children.

Ethnocentric Bible reading is so common that it is often difficult to recognize. One of the most prevalent examples in the American church is the response many Christians have when they read in the Bible about God's call to the rich and powerful to care for and serve the poor. Most people see themselves as the poor person and not the ones with social power, resources, and a safety net. It seems that for many of us in the West, the rich are only people like Bill Gates, Jeff Bezos, or the British royal family, and never people like us: those who have the funds to go to nice restaurants, travel on vacation, remodel our bathrooms, and buy a car. I believe this to be the reason that many people say we should take care of our own in need, such as military veterans and people experiencing homelessness, rather than welcome refugees and other immigrants. Bible interpretations that lead us to conclude that we are the poor and not the rich have terrible consequences for our neighbors who are marginalized, since they lead us to justify the harm done to them when we deny them entry to our countries. The implication is that countries are poor, and there is a scarcity of resources rather than an abundance. In fact, we can choose to care for all who are in need because there is more than enough for all of us, if we allocate resources in a way that prioritizes the well-being of people in vulnerable situations.

Interpretations Have Consequences

The parable of the prodigal son was instrumental in my decision to follow Jesus. I remember going to a conference as a young college student and seeing myself in the parable. I appreciated it for its simplicity and clarity. I read it like an allegory: the prodigal son represents the sinner in need of salvation; the father represents God; and the older brother represents the Pharisees and teachers of the law who did not approve of Jesus's inclusion of everyone, Jew and Gentile alike, in his mission. I was the son who wandered away from a loving father but was received in his loving arms upon my return. I never gave a second thought to the inherent antisemitism in this reading or considered that a parable is not an allegory, and I did not revisit the story again for a couple of decades, managing to avoid it even in seminary.

Imagine my shock when, as a middle-aged woman, I read Amy-Jill Levine's book *Short Stories by Jesus: The Enigmatic Parables of a Controversial Rabbi*. As a professor of both Jewish studies and the New Testament, Levine reminds readers that the parables are supposed to be unsettling—we should not be comfortable reading them.[6] She highlights the unresolved ending of this parable to illustrate this fact; the father and the older brother are engaged in an uncomfortable conversation: "The story does not end with the party, but with two men in the field, one urging and comforting, the other resisting, vacillating, or reconciled—we do not know."[7] So is it the younger brother who is lost or the older brother? Traditional interpretations say that it is the younger brother who is lost, but he has returned and is fully reconciled to his father. It is the older brother's fate that remains in question, since the parable ends without a resolution, without a reconciliation between him and his father.

Levine posits that this story is ultimately about reconciliation. The two brothers recall other pairs of brothers familiar to the original hearers of the parable: Cain and Abel, Isaac and Ishmael, and Jacob and Esau. Even Cain did not lose his life after he murdered his brother, and the other pairs of brothers were reconciled. If there is hope for them, there is hope for all our reconciliations, whether these are personal or societal.[8]

Much of the Western world displays an unwelcoming posture toward immigrants in need, and much of this hostility has been exacerbated by political leaders intent on scapegoating immigrants for their countries' problems. The church in the West should be the agent of reconciliation between the world and those on the margins—it should be like the father in the story, challenging and energizing its members to obey the God who calls them to love and welcome the immigrant in their midst. I am grieved by the knowledge that much of the church has, instead, contributed to this hostility because it has failed to teach people to locate themselves properly in the Scriptures and to understand that our interpretations have consequences. Reading the Bible responsibly means that Christians are regularly reminded of their duty to their neighbors in need; they are regularly reminded that the kind of neighbor love Christ calls us to is not easy and sentimental but costly and sacrificial.

Rather than speaking truth to white Christians about the call to love, mercy, compassion, and reconciliation, the church has become complicit in the rejection and exclusion of refugees and other immigrants. I regularly speak at churches, universities, and conferences where people ask me about Romans 13, about our duty to obey the laws of nations. Seldom am I asked about the way that Boaz in the book of Ruth obeyed not just the letter of God's law but its spirit, going above and beyond the call of duty to care for the poor immigrant widow Ruth and her elderly mother-in-law, subverting another law that said he should exclude Moabites like Ruth. But things do not have to be this way. There is still time for the church to be the agent of reconciliation between immigrants and Christians. The church can be the bridge that unites these two groups, if it accepts its role in preaching prophetically and reading the Bible from the margins instead of from places of power.

How might the American church respond to the current refugee crisis if it saw itself as Pharaoh and saw immigrants as the Hebrews living under the yoke of oppression? How might the Western church be transformed by seeing that its alliance with political power makes it more like the Roman Empire than like the early church? How might seeing rightly lead us Christians to repentance and to the work of inclusion and justice for our neighbors in vulnerable situations—the very work that Jesus modeled for us?

God of the Bible,

You've given us the Scriptures as a revelation of yourself, but we have weaponized them against our neighbors. Forgive us for our failure to read the Scriptures for the sake of the liberation of all of us. Give us new eyes to read familiar stories anew, to see and accept different perspectives that might unsettle us. It's only through your grace and truth that we can locate ourselves correctly in the Scriptures—it is only through your power that we can repent of our complicity in building systems of oppression and begin to work toward a new kind of world. Help us to reject readings that harm and exclude our immigrant neighbors. Let us become people who cling to our God and our neighbor and not to biblical interpretations passed down to us. Amen.

5

Mi Casa Es Su Casa

The Hospitality of Jesus

> If you really want to make a friend, go to someone's house and eat with him. . . . The people who give you their food give you their heart.
>
> —César Chávez

I saw Mrs. Fisher standing in the lobby before I had even exited the elevator. It was her second visit to our immigration clinic, and remembering her first, I let out an audible sigh and prepared myself to receive an earful. True to form, she let me know that she did not approve of the work my organization does to advocate for immigration policy reform.

"Why do you all have to be so political?" she asked.

I did not hide my frustration well. I chose to ignore her and focused on the other people who had come to receive a legal consultation. I collected their forms, gave them instructions, and ushered them into the elevator, where I was trapped with Mrs. Fisher, who railed against American immigration policy for two whole floors. I had scarcely led everyone to the waiting area when she began to advocate for the friend she had brought to us: "I don't think Marilú needs to see your immigration video," she said, gesturing toward the television screen. "She just needs help bringing her mother to the US."

"I understand," I replied. "But this is her first time here, correct? That means she needs to learn about the process through the video, and then she can meet with a legal practitioner to discuss her case. That's our process, and everyone has to follow it." I emphasized the word "everyone." Then I added, "You can wait at the coffee shop on the corner, if you'd prefer. There's no need for you to watch it with her."

Mrs. Fisher sat down with Marilú to watch a video in a language that was foreign to her and waited the usual two to three hours that a first consultation visit lasted.

I went back to my work, irritated that my day had started with that encounter. I struggled to understand this woman. As a professing Christian, with her gold crosses, why couldn't she see that her sneering comments were in direct opposition to the Bible's many commands to love immigrants?

Truth be told, Mrs. Fisher was an enigma to me—she expressed clear xenophobic tendencies, a fear of the "other," the foreigner, often based in ethnocentrism. But in action she was generous and even hospitable—not the hosting-a-dinner-party kind but the one described in the Bible as *philoxenia*, the love of foreigners. This love is not sentimental or a one-time act but a way of living, a code of values that involves caring for foreign people.

On her first visit, she had brought a different immigrant friend, a woman who was her housekeeper, to renew her work permit. Her friend had been putting off the renewal because she did not want to lose half a day's income by coming to see a legal adviser, so Mrs. Fisher had offered to pay her *not* to clean her house. Instead, she drove her to our immigration clinic herself, parked downtown in an expensive garage, and waited with her through the consultation. Later, she returned with her to file the actual petition. For someone who was so rabidly against welcoming immigration policies, she had given of her time, money, and other resources to assist two different people who needed immigration legal support.

I know people who verbally support refugees and other immigrants who have not done half as much to assist a single immigrant person! In my more charitable moments, she reminded me of the first son in Jesus's parable of the two sons: "A man had two sons; he went to the first and said, 'Son, go and work in the vineyard today.' He answered, 'I will not'; but later he changed his mind and went. The father went to the second and said the same; and he answered, 'I go, sir'; but he did not go" (Matt. 21:28–30).

According to Jesus's explanation in the verses that follow, it is the good deed that counts, not the yes with good intentions. Biblical scholar Richard Gardner explains, "Saying yes and doing yes would be best. Yet rebels who change their mindset and act as God requires truly fulfill God's intention. By contrast, those who piously profess to do God's will but fail to carry it out end up in the wrong."[1] Of course, this interpretation raises the question of whether Mrs. Fisher changed her mind about immigration. She was doing God's will, but did she believe God's words about welcoming and doing justice for the immigrant?

It is impossible for me to know, because I never saw her again. Yet, I would not be surprised if she had, because it has been my experience that we often practice ourselves into new ways of being and believing. I always thought that belief precedes action, and sometimes it does. But all too often, it is practices that shape us, that change our beliefs and help us internalize them in ways that are transformative. We learn by doing. I wonder if Mrs. Fisher now proclaims hospitality in addition to practicing hospitality. I hope so.

Stay with Us

I learned a lot about hospitality when I lived among Kazakh and Russian people, though most of my learning happened because of spectacular missteps both as a guest and as a host. When we arrived in Kazakhstan, my teaching partner Rebecca and I decided, as a way to get to know our students, to invite small groups of them to our apartment for tea. Every Friday, we cleaned the house, made a modified apple crisp, bought some candy, and hosted them for a couple hours of light conversation in English. I was proud of us for making this effort and felt that the gatherings were a success: we got to know them a bit better, and they got to know us as well. This satisfied feeling lasted until we were invited to the home of Galiya.

While most of our students attended the university, Galiya was much older. She was a professor at the university and quite an expert on English grammar, but she wanted to be more comfortable speaking and listening, so she signed up for our conversational English classes. She invited us to come on a Sunday for an early afternoon meal with her family, which included her husband and son. We bought a hostess gift of an inexpensive box of chocolates and headed over to her house soon after church.

I am still at a loss as to what transpired in the confusion that followed, but we mistakenly arrived at her apartment an hour early. If you have ever hosted a meal at your house, you can relate to the inconvenience of having guests show up more than a few minutes early at your door. It is simply rude. This is when the host is frantically cleaning their home, corralling their children, cooking the meal, and setting their table. Somehow, Rebecca and I, who both had analog watches, had misread the time as two o'clock when in actuality it was one.

Galiya's husband opened the door with a surprised expression. In the background, we could see her cleaning the floor of their modest flat in a housedress. I introduced myself to him in my limited Russian and stretched out my hand through the doorway. Bewildered, he quickly glanced at my face and then my hand before he decided what to do: he took my hand while walking forward, forcing me to walk backward, and pinned me against the wall of the narrow hallway. I was baffled, but I shook his hand in the small space between us. He ushered us inside where he asked Galiya to translate something for him. She told us that in their culture, it is believed that if you shake hands through a doorway, you will have an argument, which is why he had pushed me to shake hands in the hallway. I nodded my understanding and smiled, vaguely remembering having learned about this custom. Why couldn't I remember these things when it mattered?

Mortified upon realizing our mistake, Rebecca and I offered to come back in an hour, but Galiya was gracious, insisting that we stay and brought us appetizers while the meal finished cooking and her housework was complete. Soon, she joined us at the table, now wearing a dress, jewelry, and a freshly made-up face, and served us a feast. She had made traditional Central Asian dumplings, known as manty, and several salads. Bowls of succulent dishes came out of her kitchen one after the other. All of it was made from scratch by her talented hands and served on her finest dishes. The minute our plates had even the smallest space on them Galiya would scoop more food on them, encouraging, "Eat, eat! You don't eat!"

I cringed when I remembered the modest fare we had served in our own home. What must she think of our hospitality? After the meal, she served us tea, carefully filling the cups only halfway. She explained that in traditional Kazakh culture, serving tea to the brim, where it begins to get cold before you have drunk half the cup, was considered rude and inhospitable because it means you want your guests to leave. She then opened the box of chocolates we had brought, as was customary, and I was chagrined when I remembered we had not only filled all teacups to the brim at our home but also bought Galiya the cheapest box of chocolates; they cost a mere one hundred tenge, less than one US dollar. Would the humiliation never end?

We left a couple hours later, in awe of her lavish hospitality. For one whose home was so simple and modest, she had fed us and treated us as if we were royalty. And we had learned so much about our host country and its people at her feet.

Every year on one of the Sundays after Easter when a sermon is preached about the disciples on the road to Emmaus, I remember Galiya and her bountiful feast.

With Burning Hearts

What strikes me about the encounter between Jesus and his disciples on the road to Emmaus is how much it reveals about hospitality (see Luke 24:13–35). For the disciples in this Gospel text, Cleopas and his companion, it is Easter morning and they are leaving Jerusalem. Jesus's death has utterly shattered them. Who can blame them for wanting to be anywhere but there? In Jerusalem, they experienced pain, sorrow, and the tragic loss of their beloved leader. For reasons unknown to us readers, they head to a village called Emmaus, seven miles away.

As they walk, they talk about their losses, about their unmet expectations, about their disappointment. They had been so sure that Jesus was the one, but now he's dead, and with him died all their dreams. So they walk and perhaps regret their investment, the price they paid for following Jesus, because it is an investment that paid no returns. Inwardly, they are lost and untethered.

They had heard reports that the women had found an empty tomb, but that sounded like idle talk or wishful thinking. Even if true, it does not erase their losses or lessen their sadness because Jesus did not fulfill the ancient promises made to Israel. They journey on and are joined by a third companion, Jesus himself! But they don't recognize him; the text says that "their eyes were kept from recognizing him" (Luke 24:16).

This incognito Jesus asks them what they are discussing, and they relay their entire tale of woe to him. Dejected, they say, "We had hoped that he [Jesus] was the one to redeem Israel" (24:21). They must have been shocked when this stranger, this fellow traveler, responded, "Oh, how foolish you are, and how slow of heart to believe all that the prophets have declared!" (24:25). He then proceeds to interpret for them everything about himself in the Scriptures. I imagine Cleopas and his companion listening attentively to the stranger on the dry, dusty road to Emmaus and being reminded of God's faithfulness to the promises made to Israel.

But as they approach Emmaus, the stranger walks on ahead of them as if his destination is a different one than theirs. They urge him to stay with them, offering their hospitality. It is possible they want to protect him from the dangers of the night, since it is almost evening. Or perhaps something has begun to change within them in the company of this stranger. Whatever their reasons, their invitation is sincere, and they insist, so he accepts. Writer Henri Nouwen comments, "Jesus wants to be invited. Without an invitation he will go on to other places. . . . He will remain a stranger."[2] The invitation expresses a desire for a relationship—they want to be his hosts, to offer him a safe place where he can become their friend. Unbeknown to them, it is an invitation that will change everything.

This is the point where the tables quite literally turn, making Jesus the host and the disciples the guests: "When he was at the table with them, he took bread, blessed and broke it, and gave it to them. Then their eyes were opened, and they recognized him" (Luke 24:30–31). Jesus serves them a meal, and their perception changes—in the breaking of the bread their eyes are opened, and they see differently than they did before. Traditional notions of hospitality necessitate that those with means and those who extend the invitation always be the hosts, but Jesus requires *them* to be the guests; Jesus calls *them* to leave their own tables and join his.

It is noteworthy that Jesus's last act before his death is to host a meal for his disciples, the Last Supper, and that his first act after his resurrection is to host and share this "revelatory" meal.[3] "Now they [the disciples] understand why their hearts were burning as he talked to them along the road. All the scriptural and theological explanations that Jesus gave them on the road now gain new meaning. Because he has been explaining these things to them, the meal becomes particularly significant. The scriptural teaching and the meal go together; they illumine and enrich each other," says Justo González.[4]

The disciples saw and understood in the breaking of the bread when Jesus became their host. Previously, I stated how much this encounter reminded me of the meal Galiya served us in her home. What I learned from Galiya has nothing to do with extravagant hospitality or with being grateful for all the material blessings I have; that is something I could have learned in any number of places. She taught me to learn and to listen; she taught me how much she had to offer me. In one meal, I was humbled because I realized how much I had to learn: the language, the customs, the traditions, and the history of this new land. She imparted that gift to me. And that was the gift Jesus imparted to these disciples. Writer and theologian Kat Armas explains that the hospitality of Jesus is one that requires us to be "regular guests at unfamiliar tables with only the motives of listening and learning."[5]

Jesus's hospitality involves deliberate listening, learning, and engagement. That is the hospitality that Jesus gave, and that is the hospitality he affirmed when he received it.

Truthfully, there had been nothing wrong with the hospitality Rebecca and I had extended to our students, including Galiya; it was simple but sincere and given with care and affection. What I had struggled to understand is that hospitality in Kazakhstan would be reciprocal—that is, I would give it, and I would receive it. That is the hospitality of Jesus.

And that is exactly what is often missing in modern rhetoric around hospitality to refugees and other immigrants—that hospitality only moves in one direction: from the native citizen with rights to the immigrant in need. I am not referring to the kind of hospitality where an immigrant person is invited to a citizen's home for dinner, though that is one kind of hospitality. What I am referring to is the kind of hospitality that is truly engaged, where nonimmigrant Christians listen to and learn at the feet of immigrants they have welcomed to their countries—the kind where immigrants are asked to give feedback and evaluate services they receive, including resettlement; the kind where immigrants are at the table and asked to speak into the planning of programs and services that serve their own communities; the kind where their dignity and choices are respected and decisions are not made on their behalf.

When hospitality is not reciprocal, those belonging to the dominant culture unconsciously begin to think of immigrants as having less in *every* way. The truth is that immigrants may need material possessions, language classes, and other things, but as image bearers of God, we have gifts, talents, and skills, not just needs. It is important to revive the biblical practice of reciprocal hospitality in order to counteract these toxic narratives. Professor Christine D. Pohl writes, "There is a kind of hospitality that keeps people needy strangers, while fostering an illusion of relationship and connection. It both disempowers and domesticates guests while it reinforces the hosts' power, control and sense of generosity. It is profoundly destructive to the people it welcomes."[6] Without reciprocal hospitality, we unwittingly reinforce the status quo and unequal power dynamics—this action mars the image of God in our immigrant neighbors and widens the distance between us. Hosts have something to offer to immigrants, but immigrants have nothing to offer to hosts. When hospitality is reciprocal, it encourages the hosts' humility and diminishes the impact of the disparate power dynamics in the room.

Ancient Hospitality

When we hear the word "hospitality," we might initially think of holiday parties with bright decorations or fresh linens for visiting friends. Some of us might feel dread as we think about guests, even those we love, disrupting our routines and invading our spaces. We sometimes prefer to think of hospitality as a cultural value that some people are good at and others are not, thereby letting ourselves off the hook. Our modern understanding of hospitality is not as robust as it was in antiquity; it does not usually expand to include strangers and immigrants but only includes our friends and family.

That is not to say that ancient understandings of hospitality were not problematic. Greek and Roman hospitality were often offered to gain advantage, not from neighborliness, kindness, or moral obligation.[7] Hospitality was extended by a patron to a client—the client was expected to be good and worthy of hospitality and to express fawning gratitude and loyalty, much like a modern-day entourage. The entire encounter stood to benefit the patron and their reputation. Jesus challenges this understanding of hospitality in Luke 14: "When you give a luncheon or a dinner, do not invite your friends or your brothers or your relatives or rich neighbors, in case they may invite you in return, and you would be repaid. But when you give a banquet, invite the poor, the crippled, the lame, and the blind. And you will be blessed, because they cannot repay you, for you will be repaid at the resurrection of the righteous" (vv. 12–14).

In Jesus's understanding, Christian hospitality should extend to those who could not benefit you in any way—those who were poor and others on the margins of the ancient world of the first century. This hospitality was truly revolutionary because it transcended status, class, and ethnicity. Everyone was welcome in the same way.[8]

As I write these words, the Biden administration is pulling troops out of Afghanistan and attempting to evacuate American citizens as well as Afghan people who assisted the US military, now that the Taliban has taken over. Every day, I read articles, opinion editorials, and social media posts with impassioned pleas to welcome Afghan refugees for resettlement in the US. Many of these articles and posts are written by Christians who cite the biblical command to welcome and care for the refugee person in need. I fully agree with these sentiments. We must and should care for Afghan refugees.

What I struggle with is that refugees are often seen as the *only* immigrants who deserve welcome and inclusion. For political reasons, we who are migrants to the US from Mexico, Central and South America, and the Caribbean are not classified as refugees, though we flee for similar reasons: fear for our lives. We do not receive advocacy or hospitality in the same way. A biblical hospitality would demand that we receive the same welcome as refugees, but instead we are parsed and separated out, deemed undesirable immigrants. I wonder if those who write these articles and posts realize that their advocacy comes at the expense of other immigrants, because rather than extending welcome to everyone, only one group is singled out as worthy.

Our hospitality should extend to all immigrants, regardless of their manner of migration. That is the model of hospitality that Jesus set for us, countercultural and subversive. Jesus set tables where all were welcome, even when it upset those with power. He birthed an inclusive movement of justice, hope, and love with his radical and inclusive hospitality. Are we willing to do the same?

A Reimagined Hospitality

I would love to tell you that in my tiny East Coast city, lovingly called Smalltimore, I hope to run into Mrs. Fisher again so I can ask her if her views on immigration have changed, but I do not. The truth is that she bothered me; as an immigrant person, I found her words offensive. I would not blame any person who chose not to be around her and her loathsome attitude and remarks. Furthermore, as far as I could tell, her hospitality was not reciprocal—she was not engaged, listening, or learning when I encountered her.

But here is where it becomes complicated: though she was not kind or warm, she actively helped people in need to find the resources necessary to make their home in the US. Would it have been better if her hospitality had been reciprocal and accompanied by kindness and compassion? Absolutely. But all of us can likely attest to the challenges of an always joyful hospitality. In truth, there is no perfect hospitality, but we learn by doing. And there is no doubt that she was actively doing. It raises an important question: Does hospitality need to come with a smile and a warm greeting, or can it be expressed seriously in actions like voting, volunteering, donating, and driving? I believe so; there is value in giving of our time and resources to those in need. Nonetheless, we should always strive toward Jesus's model of reciprocal hospitality.

In many Latin American countries, hospitality is expressed in the familiar proverb "Mi casa es su casa." It is notable that the saying includes the pronoun "su," which stands for the formal "usted" used when talking to strangers or older people. The phrase means "My home is your home, stranger." It is an expression that is well known even in English—almost like a hospitality cliché. But like many expressions that have become clichés, we do not think much about what they are expressing or the deep truths found within them: what is mine is also yours. Make yourself at home because you are in *your* own home. There is no mine and no yours, only ours.

How does that phrase reimagine the way we think about hospitality to strangers and immigrants? How does it move us beyond the host and guest dichotomy and into reciprocal hospitality? Pastor Isaac Villegas imagines God's hospitality as his grandmother's house—"a house where there is always room around the kitchen table for another neighbor, another stranger, another guest." He continues, "God expands our vision for who are our kin, for who belongs in the household, for who can be served a bowl of arroz con pollo."[9] It is a beautiful imagining of kinship and inclusion.

I remember being awed when I learned that in his lifetime Jesus received and accepted hospitality and financial support from many people found on the margins of the first-century Near East: women, sex workers, tax collectors who were known for cheating people, and other sinners.[10] What is perhaps less known is that he also reciprocated this hospitality—though he was a man without a home as he himself says, "Foxes have holes, and birds of the air have nests; but the Son of Man has nowhere to lay his head" (Luke 9:58). He not only shared meals with people but also saw them, listened to them, accepted them, and identified fully with them. He embraced them with a hospitable generosity of heart. Listening. Learning. Engaging.

Later as he prepares for his death and for leaving his disciples, he says to them, "Do not let your hearts be troubled. Believe in God, believe also in me. In my Father's house there are many dwelling places. If it were not so, would I have told you that I go to prepare a place for you? And if *I go and prepare a place for you, I will come again and will take you to myself*, so that where I am, there you may be also" (John 14:1–3). The one who has been received, fed, cared for in many homes will now return to his home to prepare a place for them in his own Father's house—a reciprocal hospitality. They wouldn't be just guests in the house but family, welcomed in "Mi casa es su casa" style!

God our host,

In Jesus, you made your home among us in the flesh and you taught us how to give and receive hospitality. We confess we still have so much to learn from you—we don't practice hospitality to listen and learn or to engage our neighbors on the margins. Give us awareness of and keep us from a hospitality that harms and disempowers our immigrant neighbors. Let us remember the model of welcome you set for us, a hospitality that is reciprocal and empowering. Give us hearts of courage that will risk a radical hospitality. We are grateful that your Spirit makes a home within every one of us and enables us to give and receive a subversive hospitality. Amen.

The Land before (Western) Time

A Theology of Belonging

La tierra libre, la tierra para todos, la tierra sin capataces y sin amos. (The land free, free for all, land without overseers and without masters.)

—Emiliano Zapata

According to the Mayan creation myth, the deities Tepeu and Gucumatz decided to create human beings because the animals could not speak to or worship them. First, they created human beings from mud clay, but these first humans had no souls and were ugly and not well formed. They could not speak or walk, and their crumbly selves melted away in the rain.

The deities tried a second time; this time, they were determined to make a heartier race of human beings, so they created them from wood. These humans were strong and able to walk, talk, and reproduce upon the earth. However, they had no minds, no ability to show care and compassion, because their hearts were empty. They were ungrateful and unwilling to praise their creators. The deities sent a great flood to destroy them and turned creation against them—the animals attacked the surviving wood people and tore them apart. Those who managed to escape ran to the forest and became monkeys.

The deities tried again. They wanted humans who would live rightly in the world they had created. When some of the animals brought them stacks of white corn that grew on the far end of the earth, they took the corn and ground it into a paste from which they formed human beings. These beings were exactly what the deities wanted: they were hearty and strong, and their mouths praised their creators in gratitude. These people of corn were respectful of creation and walked humbly on the earth that sustained them, so they were the people allowed to remain on the earth to sustain it.[1]

Ownership and Reciprocity

When I was growing up and told my mother that I did not have energy or strength for something, she would coax me by responding playfully, "Yes, you do because you are strong. ¡Eres mujer de maíz y yo también!" (You are a woman of corn and so am I!) She would then look at me intensely and flex her bicep muscles, mockingly illustrating her tremendous strength as a mujer de maíz. Of course, she was teasing me, but this story reveals that in our collective memory as a Mesoamerican people, we are people of the land, and the Mayan creation story continues to live within us.

Robin Wall Kimmerer finds it curious that the Mayan creation myth says that people are made of corn, because corn cannot exist without human beings to tend and sow it—corn is the product of its relationship to human beings: "The sacred plant of our origin created people, and people created corn."[2] In other words, we live in reciprocity with one another, in a mutually beneficial relationship. For many years, this creation myth was interesting to me not as a point of learning about God and God's creation but as a story that is part of my ancestral heritage. Native American theologians have taught me that it can be both.

It is remarkable how little most Christians think about a theology of land and belonging when we serve the God of Israel, the God who brought the people out of slavery and into the promised land, the land flowing with milk and honey. Theologian Kat Armas notes, "Much of Israel's story is deeply rooted in land—their displacement from it and their longing to be restored to it."[3] In the New Testament, the apostle Paul recognizes that both the people and the land cry out for freedom, for liberation, because there is a divine connection between human beings, the land, and the creatures of the earth (Rom. 8:18–25).[4]

Most Christians would not dispute these connections; we affirm that God gave human beings stewardship over creation, that the gift of land comes with responsibilities as well as opportunities. And yet, our Western understanding of the world is one where humankind is the epitome of creation; perhaps this is a remnant of the humanism of the Renaissance rather than a biblical teaching. Indigenous people and theologians view the world in a different way: both human beings *and* the land are central to the creation, and they live in reciprocity—the humans take care of the land, and the land takes care of the humans by being fruitful and thus providing for their sustenance and well-being.[5] The people of corn tend and sow the corn. The land cares for the humans, and the humans care for the land. People and land are different but equally valuable in this worldview because they need one another.

Furthermore, the land does not belong to the human beings—it belongs to God, the Creator. Referencing biblical scholar Ellen F. Davis, Wendell Berry writes, "The descendants of Israel were given not a land, but the use of a land, along with precise instructions for its good care. They could keep the land only on the condition of their obedience. By their disobedience, they were estranged from the land and the covenant by which they received it, and were removed into exile."[6] The human beings are only stewards who have use of the land: "The land shall not be sold in perpetuity, for the land is mine; with me you are but aliens and tenants" (Lev. 25:23). The psalmist acknowledges this as well:

> The earth is the Lord's and all that is in it,
> the world, and those who live in it. (Ps. 24:1)

And even King David chimes in to acknowledge the Creator as the only owner of the land, and the people's status as foreigners passing through it: "For all things come from you, and of your own have we given you. For we are aliens and transients before you, as were all our ancestors; our days on the earth are like a shadow" (1 Chron. 29:14–15).

For many of us who live in the world where land is a commodity we buy and sell, it is challenging to think of all land as belonging to God. We may acknowledge it in a general sense and express gratitude to God as Creator for a beautiful landscape we encounter on a hike or see on a postcard, but ultimately the land is ours, because we do not live as if the land belongs to God alone. I sometimes try to imagine what it must have been like when the Spanish conquistadors landed on our Central American shores and claimed the land as their own. Our indigenous ancestors must have been confused since, in their understanding, only the Creator owned the land; their culture and practices did not allow for the commodifying of it.[7] Shawnee chief and warrior Tecumseh expressed that buying and selling land was akin to selling air and water.[8] How could they sell something that was lent to them by the Creator?

In the history of humankind, land has been the most important resource, one that was created for our sustenance but does not ultimately belong to us.[9] Biblical scholar Sifiso Mpofu notes, "Having been given land by God, the people of Israel entered into a covenant relationship based on 'love, justice, and equitable distribution of land amongst the twelve tribes.' . . . The people of Israel enjoyed fair and just access to land by all citizens. . . . Under this model of land access, whenever powerful citizens attempted to usurp the land of the poor, the prophets cried out and condemned their actions."[10]

God made special provisions to protect the land and, by extension, the poor from those who would behave irresponsibly and seek to hoard it. In God's economy, the land should never become a source of disillusionment, dispossession, exploitation, enslavement, or death.[11] The Scriptures say,

> The Lord enters into judgment
> with the elders and princes of his people:
> It is you who have devoured the vineyard;
> the spoil of the poor is in your houses.

> What do you mean by crushing my people,
> by grinding the face of the poor? says the Lord God
> of hosts. (Isa. 3:14–15)

Empires and Judgment

The Central Intelligence Agency (CIA) overthrew Guatemala's democratically elected president and his government in 1954.[12] The dispute was over land. Guatemala's president, Jacobo Arbenz Guzmán, proposed land reforms that were considered a threat to the interests of the United Fruit Company (UFC), a US company that had enormous economic power in Guatemala. UFC (now known as Chiquita Brands International) lobbied the US government to prevent the reforms that would have granted land to the indigenous people who worked it, because the change would have ended UFC's monopoly and exploitive labor practices. Their campaign was successful, and as the CIA was overthrowing his government in a military coup, President Arbenz resigned and fled into exile. What followed Arbenz's rule was a series of military dictators, supported by US administrations, that brought the country into a civil war resulting in the deaths of at least two hundred thousand people, most of them indigenous.[13]

This war that began over land disputes was started by one small group of wealthy Americans exploiting, dispossessing, disillusioning, and ultimately causing the deaths of poor Guatemalan indigenous people. If these privileged and powerful Americans were the wealthy and unjust of ancient Israel in the Hebrew Scriptures, God's judgment would have come down on them swiftly. Prophets would have been sent to condemn their actions and call for their repentance. The lands they took by force would have been taken from them, and they would have been exiled as punishment for disobeying their God by mistreating the poor.

We cannot seriously discuss a theology of the land and belonging without discussing the impact of empires. For ancient Israel, the oppressive empires were Egypt, Babylon, and Rome. But for many in the Global South, particularly in the Middle East, Asia, and Latin America, the oppressive empire is the United States. I was not yet born in 1954, and my parents were small children who were not even in school yet, but I am here in the US because the US was in Guatemala in 1954 overthrowing my native country's government and setting off a chain of events that resulted in a brutal civil war that eventually caused my family's migration. I am here because they were there. The American dream has become a nightmare for many in the Global South because our lives have become disposable for the sake of the comfort and well-being of the few. Our homelands are decimated, mined, and exploited to make the good life possible for people in North America.

As our countries are economically exploited and become almost unlivable, some of us migrate in search of a better life. However, life on the move does not provide the solace we seek. Biblical scholar Gemma Tulud Cruz reminds us of the injustices migrants experience in the modern world: "Today's forced migrants are like Israel in the wilderness that embarked on a journey believing that the promised land lies ahead. Unlike the Israelites, however, they do not necessarily experience their exodus as a 'justice event,' . . . since [their] quest for justice is an ongoing struggle."[14] That struggle is exacerbated by the militarization of borders that prevent us from finding our own promised land, the place where we can rest in safety and freedom.

How we view the land and theologize about it matters in the immigration conversation because it has implications for immigrants. And make no mistake, the question of immigration is ultimately one of belonging. Who belongs on the land? Who does *not* belong on the land?

Healing the Open Wound

Chicana writer and activist Gloria Anzaldúa has famously referred to the US-Mexico border as "una herida abierta [an open wound] where the Third World grates against the first and bleeds."[15] Anzaldúa herself lived in these borderlands and experienced the affliction of this open wound and the physical, economic, communal, and psychological violence it inflicts on all who inhabit it.[16] The vivid image of a gaping wound is powerful and evokes the humanitarian crisis in the borderlands. I am purposefully using the word "borderlands" rather than referring to "the border" because communities of people have lived in these lands for centuries—the imaginary line that is the border was formed much later.

My last visit to the borderlands occurred in the spring of 2019 when I found myself in El Paso, Texas, and crossed over to its Mexican neighbor, Ciudad Juárez. It is the farthest west I had ever been in Texas, and I was surprised by its sunny, dry climate, so different from the heat and humidity I had experienced in Dallas and San Antonio. The Rio Grande defines the border between these two communities to the south and west, until the river turns north. Nestled between the Hueco Mountains to the east and south, El Paso and Ciudad Juárez sit in the Chihuahuan Desert and are known locally as Paso del Norte, their historic name. It is not hard to imagine them as one big city, as they were once upon a time. But now a big gash separates them, an open wound.

Among the many myths that circulate about the borderlands is that they are places of lawlessness and horrific violence, that they are filled with chaos and crime. What I found in these communities is not what I expected to find because I believed the media and the biased political narratives too. However, I found mothers, husbands, primos, grandchildren, and tías. I saw homes, factories, supermarkets, and desert landscapes. I saw a community separated by an arbitrary line in the desert. Violent crime in the US increased in 2020, but violent crime stayed below the national average in the communities along the borderlands, around 15 percent lower. In fact, Memphis, Tennessee, a city similar in size to El Paso, had a violent crime rate that was seven times higher than El Paso's.[17]

Across the bridge in Ciudad Juárez, Mexico, things feel similar, though it is a visibly poorer area. Because Ciudad Juárez is known as one of the most violent cities in the world, I did not know what to expect, but I was pleased to see that there is a large and uneventful movement of people between the two cities every day. The murders that have made the city well known are overwhelmingly drug-cartel related and are mostly limited to certain parts of the city.[18] One notable difference between the two cities are pink crosses that we encountered throughout Ciudad Juárez and on the hillsides; each of these serves as a grim reminder of a missing or murdered girl or woman from the area. Since 1993, more than six hundred women and girls have been tortured, raped, and murdered in and around Ciudad Juárez, and many more of them are missing.[19] Most were working poor women, employed in the maquiladoras (factories) on the Mexican side of the border. Foreign companies own these factories that create products for export with inexpensive Mexican labor. The pink crosses serve as a form of resistance and proclaim that these women will not be forgotten.

I did not cross the border on my own but with a group of mostly white Christians interested in learning from, advocating for, and standing in solidarity with immigrants. They were all people who recognized the injustices that are part of everyday life in the borderlands: the inability to move across the border and access resources or be reunited with family members. We visited migrant shelters in Ciudad Juárez that are run by different churches, both Protestant and Roman Catholic, and we encountered migrants from Central America and Cuba.

I will admit that as an immigrant I was a bit uncomfortable with this trip—I saw myself and my own family in the faces of the immigrants we met and felt that we were consuming their trauma and pain. It was unsettling for me to gather around immigrants while they told stories of their suffering as they waited in limbo, because I knew that lots of groups like ours had visited them and that they had shared these painful stories over and over. I know learning is important but not at the cost of human dignity and well-being. Nevertheless, I was on this trip as well, so I could not stand in judgment of my fellow travelers; I simply tried to mitigate the harm. The immigrants were generous and shared parts of their stories with us, including the harrowing journey to Ciudad Juárez—we listened. We heard about the drug cartels, the preying on migrants because they likely carry cash, the exorbitant cost of hiring a coyote (human smuggler), the waiting on asylum cases, and their hopes that North Americans would see the humanity they share with immigrants.

I could see that many in our visiting group were touched by these stories. They asked thoughtful questions and listened attentively. Some were overcome with emotion, with despair and hopelessness.

On our way back to El Paso, we did not cross on foot but in a van that drove us across the bridge. We talked openly about what we had seen, heard, and experienced. Everyone discussed the importance of advocating, of discipling the white evangelical church, of putting pressure on our legislators to reform the immigration process and have more welcoming policies, of sharing these stories with their churches and friends back home. Notably, nobody questioned what was to me the most obviously problematic aspect of the situation: a society that had made us believe that those migrants did not belong in the US unless they entered through a proper legal process, that they were trying to access a land that belonged to other people. The driver of the van, Elias, was born in El Paso to Mexican parents and had been raised traveling back and forth between El Paso and Ciudad Juárez, having family in both cities. He was timid and mentioned quietly that all of this land was once connected and was settled by indigenous people. When European settlers arrived, it was still one community, until the border was built right through it, right through El Paso del Norte.

Anzaldúa is right about the border itself; it is an open wound that sheds blood day after day with impunity. It separates families and communities, creates the opportunity for exploitation and criminality, and causes death and destruction. The border is the enemy, not the people who inhabit the borderlands. Theologian Justin Ashworth notes, "The barbwire fence first pierces the earth before it pierces those who crawl under it."[20] It harms both land and people. How do we heal this open wound?

In the Gospel of Luke, Jesus illustrates what it means to love your neighbor when he tells the story of a Samaritan man who encountered a foreign man on the road. This man had been beaten and robbed (Luke 10:25–37). It is noteworthy that the Samaritan does not walk by the wounded man and forget him, even though he is a stranger from another ethnic group. The Samaritan also does not stop to pray for him or to consider advocating for safer roads to Jericho before he moves along to his destination. He feels compassion and takes full responsibility for the hurt stranger; he tends to his wounds, bandages them, and then picks him up and takes him to an inn, where he takes care of him and pays the innkeeper to look after him. The Samaritan practices a holistic ethic of love for his neighbor, one that is costly and sacrificial, not sentimental and convenient. He bandages wounds he did not inflict.

Bringing healing to the earth and to immigrants in the borderlands will be similarly costly and sacrificial. It will require us to follow immigrants rather than lead them: "Perhaps the very act of sneaking under this thin edge of barbwire, of transgressing this unnatural boundary, is God's way of inviting us to participate in God's healing of wounds."[21] After all, God has always worked through unlikely heroes, the ones rejected by those in power, the ones we least expect to lead movements and bring about transformation. Perhaps they will be the ones to bring healing to the wounded earth; perhaps they will save native citizens from the judgment that awaits those who ignore the plight of the wounded and go about their days (Luke 16:19–23).[22] Perhaps rather than condemn immigrants who enter the country unlawfully, we should applaud them for subverting an unjust system, for obeying God's laws above human-made ones.

In his book *Embracing Hopelessness*, biblical ethicist and scholar Miguel De La Torre discusses a theology and ethics para joder, a crude, informal way of expressing in Spanish a theology of messing with the system—essentially, a theology that says, "Screw it." For De La Torre, an ethics para joder is a practice of liberation by which society is transformed because screwing with the immigration system and the way it prevents access to land and resources is the only ethical response "in the hope of creating new opportunities through disorder and chaos."[23]

Under this ethical framework, immigrants swim across the Rio Grande and enter the country without being admitted, subverting US laws. This ethic might also lead citizens to help immigrants who are undocumented—to bring them water in the desert, to shelter and feed them by providing sanctuary in their churches, and to help them as they seek to reunite their families. Native citizens might also block the ICE agents' vehicles to keep them from taking away and deporting their immigrant neighbors. Citizens might also do what a group of over six hundred people, mostly women, did to protest former president Trump's "zero tolerance" stance on illegal immigration: sit on the floor of the Senate office building wrapped in metallic silver blankets similar to those given to migrant children separated from their families at the US-Mexico border.[24]

Immigrants and citizens come together to screw with the system, and they stop simply hoping that the system will change and become more just. The kind of hope that keeps one waiting for change, says De La Torre, can be oppressive and prevents us from seeking creative solutions and new possibilities when confronting an oppressive system.[25] Make no mistake, however: an ethics para joder is not anarchy or stealing land back but rather "a non-violent survival strategy based on love designed to liberate the abused from death-dealing social structures that deny their humanity, and the abusers whose own humanity is lost through their complicity with these same structures."[26]

Healing the open wound will also require paying reparations because countries in the Global South are not poor; they have been looted for the enrichment of other countries. The Samaritan took full financial responsibility for wounds he did not cause; he restored a stranger to health at his own expense. What are North American and European countries willing to do? What are white Christians willing to advocate for?

At the end of the parable, Jesus tells the lawyer, "Go and do likewise," meaning to show mercy and care to your neighbor as the Samaritan did (Luke 10:37). Centering immigrants in the immigration conversation means that we reevaluate how we think about land and belonging. It requires us to stand in opposition to Western empires and to proclaim that the land is for all of us; we do not accept and enforce the empire's status quo, and we do not settle for systems of injustice because that is the way things have always been. God meant this world to be different, and it is our duty to bring about the vision of creation God intended—the one where the land has no owner but God and we live in reciprocity, taking care of the land as it takes care of us. We heal the wounded earth by bringing down the walls, the barbed wire, and the fences that pierce it. This work begins with our own paradigm shift—we have accepted borders and the violence associated with them as normal, but what if we envisioned lands without borders? What if all of us envisioned the earth as truly belonging to God? What if we reimagined our relationship to land?

I used to believe those kinds of questions were idealistic and unhelpful. After all, we live in a reality where borders exist and have for a long time. Nevertheless, I am also aware of how societal shifts happen, and they begin with ideas and conversations that change the narrative. I remember being in Puebla, Mexico, in 1990 and reading a sign at a university that announced a seminar on Christopher Columbus's *invasion* of America—not "discovery" but "invasion." I had never encountered such language, and it seemed ludicrous to me to host a seminar on something that would never change in the court of public perception or opinion.

But just forty years later, a historically insignificant number of years, we have state governments in the US replacing Columbus Day with Indigenous Peoples' Day; we have statues of Columbus defaced, beheaded, or destroyed; and we have a changing narrative that focuses on the actual history surrounding Columbus's trips to the Americas and the genocide of indigenous communities. Even in white Christian spaces, people are recognizing the enormous harm unleashed by Columbus and his invasion—churches pray for the healing and restoration of indigenous communities, and Christians openly critique the history we were taught about Columbus's heroism. Change can and does happen, but it requires us to take the first step of reimagining the world and changing the narrative.

Frequently, well-meaning white Christians ask me if I believe in open borders. The question is asked almost like a litmus test—is this woman much too radical for me to engage her on the subject of immigration? I answer this question carefully—I usually say that in an ideal world, I would, but in the world we live in, I know it may not happen. But why is it radical to believe in open borders? Why is it radical to proclaim that the earth is the Lord's?

White Christians are right to be concerned about land and borders, but their concern should be about whether preventing movement across borders to access resources is biblical. Our concern should be about whether borders are just, whether it is a good use of our time to advocate for secure borders rather than for their erasure. If the land belongs to God, we have no right to prevent God's children from moving in and out of it for their well-being. Of course, North America is not a theocracy. Most North Americans live in republics, and like all people who live in republics, Christians in North America have the right to pressure their legislators for policies and laws that align with their values. The question is whether their values align with their God or with the empire.

It has become customary now to open conferences and services with land acknowledgments—that is, acknowledging the indigenous people who were displaced when European settlers took ownership of the land. Land acknowledgments are important because they remind all of us that the first displaced people on the American continents were indigenous people, but in my opinion, they should go a bit further. They should also remind all of us who follow the God-man Jesus who walked the earth that the land is not a commodity to buy and sell but a gift from our Creator for us to steward. They should acknowledge that God gave us all fair access to land for our good, so the land would be a source of life, sustenance, freedom, and hope.

God of land,

We have been looking for place and belonging ever since Adam and Eve were cast out of Eden. In our search, we've lost our connection to the land—we have not stewarded the land that belongs to you. Instead, we have exploited it as well as our neighbors. Free us from our tendency to see land as a commodity rather than a gift from you, our Creator. In your mercy, bring us back to a vision of land as a source of life and well-being for all of us, not just a few. Remind us of the gift of reciprocity where we care for the land, and the land cares for us. Above all, make us people who are generous with what you have freely given us, including the land and its resources. Give us the courage to reimagine the world around us. Amen.

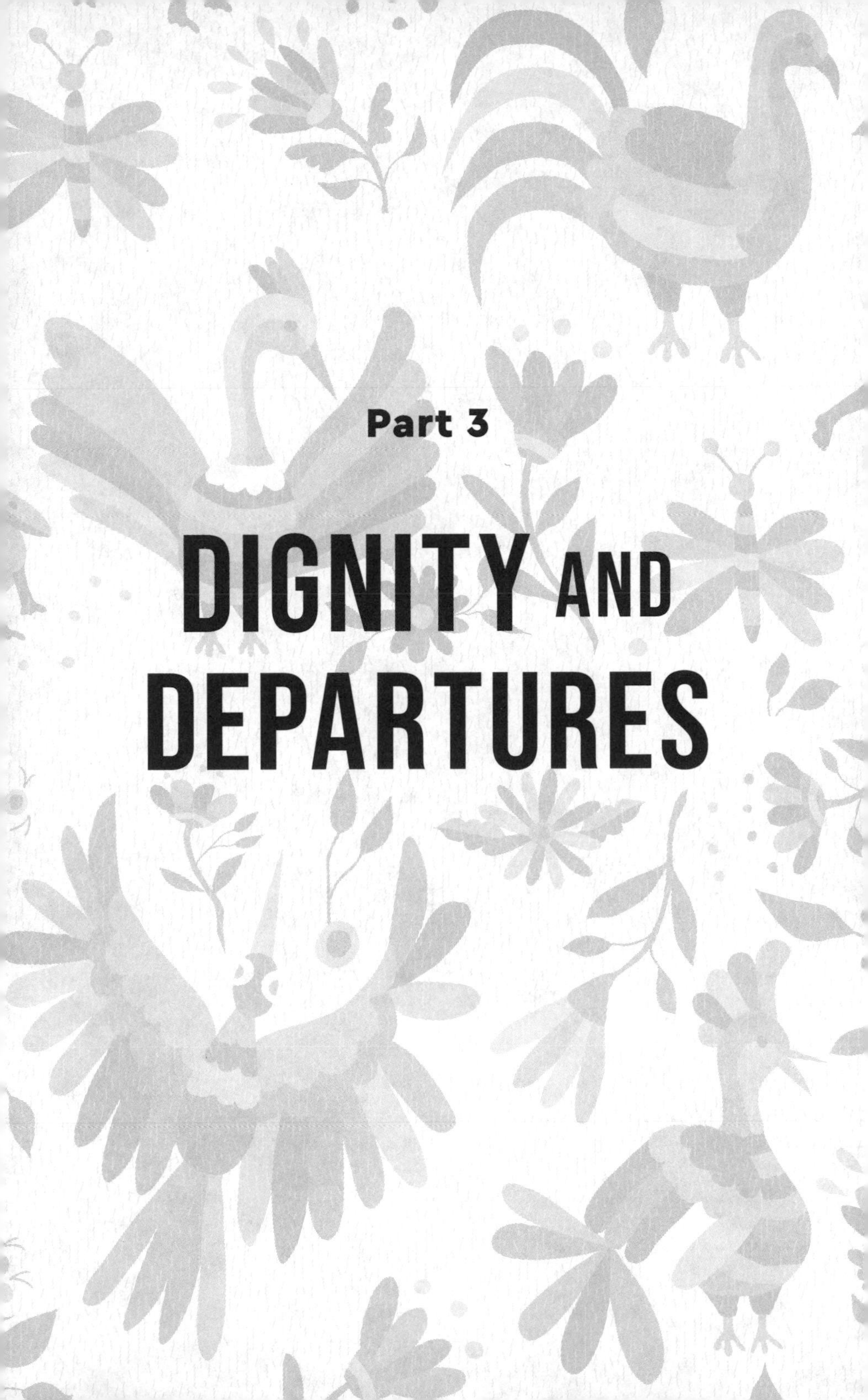

Part 3

DIGNITY AND DEPARTURES

7 Departures

People on the Move

> For God does not create a longing or a hope without having a fulfilling reality ready for them. But our longing is our pledge, and blessed are the homesick, for they shall come home.
>
> —Isak Dinesen, *Anecdotes of Destiny and Ehrengard*

We had exactly twelve hours to spend in Dublin, Ireland. We calculated that if transport from the airport to the city took forty-five minutes each way, we actually had about ten hours to do a little exploring. I was traveling to France and Italy with my father and siblings—it was our gift to our father for his seventieth birthday, and we had flown out of New

England five hours earlier. We were exhausted, but we had to venture into the city for our long layover.

To be perfectly candid, I am not one of those people who dreamed all their lives of visiting Ireland; perhaps that is why it was not a destination that made it on our itinerary. Unlike many of my neighbors on the East Coast, I have no roots there whatsoever, and, therefore, no romantic connection to its immigrants arriving on a boat, weary but hopeful, at Ellis Island.

All I really knew about the place I had learned in the fifth grade, when my teacher came to school donning an old green sweater and a leprechaun hat and told us that his name was no longer Mr. Greenberg but Mr. O'Greenberg. That day, my classmates playfully pinched me because I had not worn green, and I was bewildered because I could not remember a single instance in my Catholic childhood where we had observed Saint Patrick's feast day. Who was this Saint Patrick? Mr. Greenberg taught us about a terrible potato famine in Ireland that resulted in many deaths and in mass immigration to the US. Our day ended with the school librarian reading us a story about Saint Patrick driving all the snakes out of Ireland. Such was my limited knowledge about the Emerald Isle.

I nodded off on our way to the Dublin city center and woke up to an overcast rainy day. We had until lunch to walk around before meeting my old campus pastor near the Dublin Docklands. We strolled to Trinity College and saw the Book of Kells, the illuminated manuscripts of the Gospels. It was insanely crowded, and we found it hard to enjoy our visit, but venturing outside in the rain did not seem appealing in the least. Around noon, we abandoned our browsing around the long room of the college library and began our slow walk toward the Docklands. My friend had told me to meet him at a place called

EPIC, but during our walk I received a message that he could not make it; something had come up suddenly. We decided to head there anyway.

On our walk, we encountered a set of bronze statues just across the street from the EPIC building. These were not the kinds of statues that commemorate a victory in battle or honor a great leader or activist; they were unusual because they portrayed poor people, emaciated to the point of death. The sad, haunting figures carry belongings and even another human being in need who is not able to walk on their own. Their weariness reveals that the journey to the Docklands had been long and grueling; some died along the way. Still, they trudged along toward an unknown destination. A plaque informed us that they are called *The Famine Sculptures*, a monument to the many citizens who fled Ireland, some at that very dock on a ship called *Perseverance*, and headed to North America in search of literal greener pastures after the Great Famine. It was strange and surreal to encounter them while on vacation. They were not monuments to consume and capture in photographs but rather to meditate on, to reflect on human resilience and suffering.

Suddenly in a somber mood that was no doubt exacerbated by exhaustion and jet lag, I trailed behind my family as we entered the building. I had lost all enthusiasm and energy for sightseeing, but my interest was piqued by a museum at this very location. As it turns out, EPIC is the location of the Irish Emigration Museum. This museum was not concerned with immigration, defined as people moving *into* a country, but with emigration, people migrating *out* of one—in this case, out of the Republic of Ireland. It covers the Irish diaspora and emigration to other countries from about 500 CE to the present day. Our visit coincided with the publication of my first book on faith and migration, so I was fascinated. I was sorry that I would not get to see my campus pastor, but it seemed absolutely providential that he had led us here.

We walked inside and found ourselves in a small room that announced that migration is natural and has always occurred. People have been migrating in and out of Ireland for as long as its history has been recorded. On the wall, a giant map revealed all the sea routes in and out of the small island country. The museum boasted of the contributions that Irish immigrants had made in their host countries, particularly to the United States, Canada, and Australia. US president John F. Kennedy had Irish ancestry; so did the American writer F. Scott Fitzgerald and the Hall of Fame baseball player Connie Mack. Every room in the museum emphasizes that migration is not about what you leave behind but about what you bring to your new country.

In Search of Place

It has been said that human beings have been looking for place, and for belonging, ever since Adam and Eve were cast out of Eden. Displacement is one of the tragedies that befell the first humans in the biblical narrative; they lost not only their perfect communion with God but also their perfect home. So they traveled east in search of a new home. Scripture says that no matter where they made their home now, life would be hard because something had been broken, and it affected every sphere of life—the land they would work for their survival would now be full of thorns and thistles, and they would struggle for sustenance. The search for place, for belonging and well-being, would become part of the human experience.

Adam and Eve's son Cain received the harshest punishment for murdering his brother, Abel: displacement. He cries out to God, "Today you have driven me away from the soil, and I shall be hidden from your face; I shall be a fugitive and a wanderer on the earth" (Gen. 4:14). He can think of no greater loss than the loss of home, but God is undeterred by his cries, and Cain accepts his fate. Eventually, he settles in the land of Nod.

Adam's descendant Noah migrates under the most unusual circumstances: a flood over the whole earth. Later, Scripture says that as people migrated from the east, they settled in the land of Shinar and built a city and the Tower of Babel: "So the Lord scattered them abroad from there over the face of all the earth, and they left off building the city" (Gen. 11:8).

By the time we are introduced to the patriarch Abram/Abraham in Genesis 12, the Lord has asked him to migrate. At the age of seventy-five, he departs Haran for the land of Canaan and settles there for a time. When famine strikes, he migrates yet again, this time to Egypt in search of food. He then returns to Canaan with his wife and a young Egyptian woman named Hagar.

Jacob and his eleven sons suffer a different famine, and they, too, migrate from Canaan to Egypt, where they prosper and grow into a nation (Gen. 42–47). After generations of oppression (Exod. 1), God delivers the Hebrews from slavery in the events of the miraculous exodus (Exod. 15). They cross the Red Sea only to find themselves wandering in the wilderness—free but lost, without a place, without a home.

After decades in the wilderness, the Israelites long for a place of their own so much that they do not hesitate to displace the Canaanites and claim the land flowing with milk and honey as their own (Josh. 2). It does not enter their consciousness to consider that their gain is the loss of someone else's home. They enter and take possession of the land, grateful to have a place to rest at last.

We do not have the eyes to see it, nor have we been given the lenses to see it in many of our churches. But the Scriptures are ripe with stories of the movement of people, sometimes by choice, sometimes by calling, and sometimes by difficult circumstances. It is noteworthy that the sacred text casts no judgment on those who migrate. And human movement is not treated as unusual or undesirable in the Bible but merely as a normal part of life. People migrate, and that is a fact.

An Open Land

When I was a teenager learning American history, our textbook began by telling us that the first North American was an immigrant—not the first European but the first indigenous North American. Long ago, because nobody knows exactly when, indigenous people had likely walked across the frozen Bering Strait from the Russian Far East into what is now Alaska. Eventually, they and other migrants made their way south from Alaska and Canada all the way to the countries known today as Chile and Argentina in South America and settled all throughout the Americas.

I thought of this often during the years I spent in Kazakhstan teaching English as a volunteer with a Christian organization. Kazakhs were a nomadic people before their country aligned itself with its northern neighbor, Russia, and eventually became part of the Soviet Union. They would migrate in search of land where their horses and other animals could graze; that is why there are not many ancient settlements in the vast steppes of the country and into Siberia to the north. Many Kazakh cities were founded after the country became part of the Soviet Union because it was only then that their nomadic life ended.

Some of the indigenous tribes in North America were nomadic as well. I discovered this in middle school when I wondered aloud where the North American indigenous tribes built their pyramids. I knew the Aztecs and the Mayans had built cities and temples; I had visited them as a little girl in my native Guatemala and in Mexico. My teacher offered that many North American tribes were nomadic and did not build large settlements like the ones I had seen. Nomadic people, she taught us, go wherever their needed resources are—they come and go with the seasons.

Movement is natural. People have migrated whenever they have had an open land and the right to move—and even when they haven't. After my parents received the right to permanent legal residency in the US, they chose to leave our home in Southern California in search of a place where property prices were more affordable. They did not call it "migration" because that is not how people typically refer to movement when it occurs within a country, but we migrated from the West to the East Coast. We arrived just after the Mariel boatlift that brought thousands of Cuban refugees to South Florida.

On my most recent visit to Guatemala, I reconnected with my cousin Evelyn. She no longer lives in Guatemala City. She and her husband migrated to Zacapa, another municipality within the country about two hours away, close to the border with El Salvador. Evelyn and her husband struggled to make a living in Guatemala but did not want to leave their native country, so when an opportunity arose in another part of the country, they packed up their young family and made a new life in Zacapa. There, they became entrepreneurs, starting two different businesses they still run today.

In my adult life I have spent time living in Mexico, Kazakhstan, and Russia. Within the United States, I have lived in California, Florida, Oklahoma, Rhode Island, and now Maryland. I have moved for jobs, for education, for family, and even for no reason at all. The fact is that the land is open, and picking up everything and moving feels natural to me, as natural as some people feel about staying in one place all their lives.

Science journalist Sonia Shah says that it is easy enough for us to be lulled into the false perception that immigrant movement is the exception to the rule—that what is normal is to stay in one place.[1] She adds, "But life is on the move, today as in the past. For centuries, we've suppressed the fact of the migration instinct, demonizing it as a harbinger of terror. We've constructed a story about our past, our bodies, and the natural world in which migration is the anomaly. It's an illusion. And once it falls, the entire world shifts."[2] Today, more people than ever live outside of their country of origin and do so for varied reasons.[3] The twenty-first century has been dubbed "the age of migration," since immigrants make up 3 percent of the world's population. While that number sounds small, it represents 244 million people. Were they to gather in one place, they would make up the world's fifth most populous nation.[4] What is unnatural, then, is not movement or migration but the restriction or prevention of movement.

Climate Refugees

The road to Panajachel from Guatemala City is winding and long; it requires traversing mountains. Because of my tendency toward experiencing motion sickness, I found myself staring out the front passenger window at the birds in the sky, wishing I could travel there as they did: in one direct flight, high above these nauseating hairpin curves.

But it is also a beautiful drive with breathtaking overlooks, verdant landscapes, and volcanoes spewing fire and black, billowy smoke. Dizzy and nauseated as I felt, I recalled an old song by Gloria Estefan about nostalgia for one's home country, even a place where you did not spend very much time. I experienced pangs of longing for this place and faint regret about having spent so little time in Guatemala.

As we approached our destination, the scenic drive took us through many cafetales (coffee plantations). I knew about these, not from my memories of this place but, strangely enough, from Starbucks. They sell an Atitlán coffee that comes from this region. I told my companions in the car about Starbucks' Guatemalan coffee, and so we decided to stop at one of the myriad stands along the road to buy some coffee beans and perhaps some spiced hot chocolate to drink, cocoa being another specialty grown here.

The weather was unusually warm for December. We had all expected colder weather, remembering the brisk mountain air of this region, and I immediately regretted my jeans and sweatshirt as I exited the car. My Tía Pía pulled out a handheld fan from her purse as we walked around. The stands overlooked majestic Lake Atitlán, surrounded by green mountains. The smell of sweet cocoa and cinnamon wafted in the air. My brother intended to buy a lot of coffee, so I made light conversation with a vendor.

"¡Que calor!" I exclaimed. "This weather is not what I expected."

"It's normal now," he replied, pointing his chin toward the lake and mountains behind him. I must have looked puzzled, because he added, "It used to be so cold here, but the weather has become warmer and warmer. The cafetales are moving higher because the land is changing and coffee needs cold." I knew that he referred to Guatemalan cold, cardigan and closed-toe-shoe cold, not January-in-Toronto cold. But there was no doubt that this was dry, hot weather. Coffee is one of the many crops endangered by climate change, and experts say that as much as 88 percent of the coffee-growing land in Latin America could be unproductive by the year 2050.[5] The rising temperatures bring droughts, increase the risk of diseases that affect coffee plants, and kill the insects that pollinate the plants.[6]

Climate change is affecting not just the land but also the people who live on it. Devastating fire seasons ravage anything in their path; droughts last so long the earth cracks like an eggshell and refuses to produce; tropical storms and hurricanes destroy homes and villages with their winds and floods as if they were made of toothpicks. Such conditions have created climate refugees, even in North America. We have seen thousands leave New Orleans after the floods and destruction of Hurricane Katrina and settle in other parts of the country. Others have migrated out of California and other West Coast states, fleeing the fires that threaten and consume homes. People have abandoned entire towns at risk from fires in favor of safer places.

Between 2008 and 2014, climate change accounted for twenty-six million people on the move around the world.[7] It is a shocking statistic for those of us who live in cities in the West and do not depend on working the land day by day for our survival, who have a safety net and make our living sitting at desks and working at computers. The land is changing, usually not for the better. Its transformation is displacing people who can no longer live off that land.

It makes me wonder what Panajachel might look like in thirty years and what will happen to its people. Coffee is Guatemala's major export and makes up 40 percent of its agricultural revenue. It is grown in twenty of its twenty-two departments or regions.[8] And it is not just a crop that supports the economy; it is also an integral part of our culture. We drink coffee at or after almost every meal, often accompanied by pan dulce; cafecito is central to our sobremesas, or post-meal conversations. It is reasonable to assume that the collapse of the industry would have devastating effects on the country, the culture, and its people and may very well result in forced migration.

Naturalization

My mother never really liked cooking. She resented the way that patriarchal norms had relegated women to the kitchen and launched her own quiet resistance by cooking only on occasion and not being especially good at it. There was one exception: chirmol. Chirmol is an integral part of Guatemalan cooking; it is to Guatemalans what chimichurri is to Argentineans. It is a fresh and delicious sauce that serves as the topping for carne asada or any Guatemalan churrasco (barbecue). It consists of only the following ingredients: tomatoes, onion, mint, cilantro, lime juice, bird's eye chilies, and salt.

When we moved to the US, my mother lamented that customs would not allow her to bring in mint or cilantro plants. She did not know if she would be able to find them in the US, so she wanted to plant them herself. As it turns out, it did not matter since we arrived in Rhode Island in the winter and were greeted by snowy landscapes, unfriendly to plants in need of warmth and sun.

Later, when we moved to Florida and into a predominantly white community, she could rarely find these herbs in the grocery store, though sometimes they were hidden in the back of the produce section where only the workers could go. She hated bothering them, but she would ask them to check to see if any cilantro or mint were stored in the back and out of sight. Were she alive today, she would marvel that they are now available in vast quantities in every grocery store.

She finally found the aromatic herbs in a nursery and planted them in big pots in the screened porch behind our house. She tended to the little plants with love and care, excited to see the cilantro plant sprout flat, feathery leaves. And she made chirmol to her heart's content, harvesting the leaves as needed and being careful not to uproot the little plants. My father would grill the carne asada, and she would put together the chirmol for all of us to enjoy.

I discovered as an adult that while the tomato is native to Latin America, cilantro is not. As integral as cilantro is to so many of our dishes, it was imported. The herb originated in southern Europe and North Africa, and Europeans brought it to the Americas in the 1600s. In Europe, it is still known strictly as coriander, but the Spanish translation of coriander is cilantro. I find it strange even to think of so many of our native dishes without cilantro; in fact, the very smell of it cooking in broth activates a sensory memory and takes me back to childhood meals at home enjoying hearty and delicious caldos (soups) with meat and vegetables.

To me, cilantro feels native to Latin America because it has become naturalized to us. It was once a foreign herb but, over time, was integrated into our cooking and eventually found a place of real belonging, bringing unique flavor and aroma to our national foods. This immigrant plant made itself at home among us. I cannot imagine that anyone knows when the change took place, when it transitioned from immigrant to native, but it happened; it became a part of our culinary landscape. Perhaps it feels strange to refer to a plant as an "immigrant," because that is a word we reserve for people on the move. But just like an immigrant, cilantro has pledged itself to us, and now it is ours, an honored member of our communities.

When I pick up a fragrant bunch of cilantro in the grocery store, I sometimes think about how I became naturalized too. When I was eighteen, my father filled out the Application for Naturalization (N-400) on my behalf. We had become permanent US residents six years earlier and could now apply for citizenship. I thought there might be something romantic about a petition that bears an evocative name like "naturalization." But it is just a basic immigration application, though perhaps longer and more tedious than others. A petitioner has to meet many requirements. Among them are

proving they are able to read, write, and speak basic English;
showing they have a general understanding of US history and government;
showing they have not spent more than a year outside the US; and
showing they are a person of good moral character.

Essentially, you prove to the US government that you have become naturalized to this country before they make it official:

you speak the language; you know the rules, and you follow them; and this is your home—you do not live anywhere else most, if not all, of the time. Most people prove they have good moral character by providing copies of their income taxes for the previous five years. These copies reveal not only that they follow the law but that they are committed to supporting the social structures and systems of the country. All of that, in the government's estimation, makes you naturalized.

Writer and scientist Robin Wall Kimmerer describes naturalization this way: "Being naturalized to a place means to live as if this is the land that feeds you, as if these are the streams from which you drink, that build your body and fill your spirit. To become naturalized is to know that your ancestors lie in this ground. Here you will give your gifts and meet your responsibilities. To become naturalized is to live as if your children's future matters, to take care of the land as if our lives and the lives of all our relatives depend on it."[9]

This is what immigrants do, wherever their displacement takes them, and no matter the reason. They become naturalized, grafted into our communities like a vine or a plant. Immigrants contribute to the flourishing of life wherever they are displaced. At the Irish Emigration Museum, I was in awe of the fact that Irish people understood this so well—how natural and normal migration is, a view North Americans would do well to adopt. My father offered the gentle reminder that the Irish might be so positive regarding immigration because the migration had been out of their country, not into it. Perhaps that is true, but I hope not. I hope they really do believe in the natural force for good that is immigration. On our way out, we learned that EPIC stands for "Every Person Is Connected."

Embracing a New Citizenship

The apostle Paul uses various metaphors to communicate Christian ideas about salvation and sanctification. In his letter to the Philippians, he uses the metaphor of citizenship to explain that it does not matter if a person is a citizen of Rome; what matters is being a citizen of heaven, because our salvation is found in that lasting kingdom, a far superior one than Rome. We are, Paul wrote, citizens with the saints and members of the household of God: "Our citizenship is in heaven, and it is from there that we are expecting a Savior, the Lord Jesus Christ" (Phil. 3:20). Biblical scholar Moisés Silva emphasizes that what is most important to Paul, who is himself a Roman citizen, is that we as Christians exhibit "citizenlike behavior," which is only possible because followers of Christ have heavenly power.[10]

When people discuss citizenship in an earthly nation, many often refer to the rights and responsibilities of a citizen. For example, the US government obligates its citizens to pay taxes, obey laws, and contribute to American society. Paul, however, turns this idea on its head. Instead of pointing out our obligations as citizens of the kingdom of heaven, he stresses that it is precisely our citizenship in this different kind of kingdom that gives us the hope to be able to live a life worthy of the gospel, a life in which our values are aligned with Christ's.[11] In other words, our citizenship in the kingdom of heaven does not take from us but gives us the ability to live rightly and justly in the world, even when it opposes the empire.

In our churches today, when we reinforce Paul's exhortation to remember our citizenship in heaven, it is almost always in the context of the next life. We are reminded that the troubles of this life will pass, and we will enter the kingdom of heaven. But Paul's use of this metaphor was to keep believers' eyes focused not only on the next world but also on this one. In the context of the immigration conversation, what does it mean to live as if we are citizens of the kingdom of heaven? What should American, Canadian, or German citizenship mean to those who follow Jesus? For those of us who are foreigners passing through this world, what is our responsibility to those who cross earthly borders?

Thinking of Christian believers as foreigners raises the question of how we as foreigners should engage immigration in general. When immigration is discussed in Christian circles, it is still often considered an anomaly, something unusual that is not desirable or the norm. It is seen as another social issue that believers should engage. Perhaps if we took Paul's words to heart and truly saw ourselves as foreigners, too, we would engage immigration and immigrants in a different way; we might remember that the only citizenship that ultimately matters is the one in the kingdom of heaven. The values of that kingdom dictate that loving God and loving our neighbor are the highest commandments. Everything else is secondary, even protecting nations, languages, and cultures.

It is noteworthy that people do not even consider migration within North America as real migration—even though North Americans move within their own borders for the same reasons people have always moved: jobs, family, and safety and security. I wonder how attitudes in the church might change if we taught not only how much movement of people there is in the Scriptures but also how much there is today, even within North America, and how incredibly normal it is to migrate in search of place. If the church in North America is to have immigrant-centered immigration ministries, it has a duty to normalize migration—to emphasize that movement is natural and a fundamental human right. Let us work toward an understanding of Paul's citizenship model that will shape the church and conform its image to Christ's own.

God of departures,

Thank you for being the God of movement and belonging. We confess that we have created a world in which there are native citizens on the inside and immigrants on the outside. We are grateful that in the Scriptures you reveal to us the normalcy of movement, that in its pages we find people who moved for the same reasons people still move today. Help us to internalize the words of Paul, to know deep in our hearts that the only citizenship that matters is in the kingdom of heaven. As much as we long for place, we need you to show us how to make room for others. Expand our vision, our sense of family and country, our knowledge that ultimately we all belong to you, not to the places where we happened to be born. Give us eyes to see the human movement in our midst. As we find ourselves in a time of growing nationalism and xenophobia, give us the courage to reject these narratives and instead to reimagine our world, to bring one into being where everyone belongs, where all can become naturalized and included. Amen.

Ethical Storytelling

Disrupting the Narrative

> Tell me a fact and I'll learn. Tell me a truth and I'll believe. But tell me a story and it will live in my heart forever.
>
> —Native American Proverb

"I wrote about you in my newsletter," she said.

"Oh?" I responded curiously.

"How you've come such a long way in your relationship with God. I didn't know if you'd make it. Honestly, I questioned it. But I wrote about you going overseas as a missionary and the part the ministry played in all of it."

I nodded and changed the subject. I was having a conversation with a staff member from the college ministry group I had joined at my university. I had continued volunteering with the ministry past my graduation date and remained connected to the staff and students. I will admit that the road had been bumpy. On the one hand, this group felt like family at times, the family I felt I lost when my mother died. On the other hand, I was deeply afraid of being known because I had the sense that parts of me would not be welcome in that space, so I never brought my whole self to them. I knew that my feelings of belonging hinged on a particular identity that I had to portray—it was fragile belonging. Moreover, I was still dealing with the grief and trauma of my childhood and losing my mother. Trauma waits for stillness to reveal itself, and my college years had been the closest thing I had had to stillness.

Now it had been several years since I had actively volunteered with the ministry, so I was curious. What had been written about me? In addition, why had she written about me without asking me? She apparently thought there was nothing wrong with what she had written because she had told me about it. We had a mutual friend from church, so I was able to get my hands on a copy of the newsletter and read it.

I hold stories as sacred and personal, so it felt like a violation to read her interpretation of my story. She shared things I had told her in conversations just between the two of us, and she had compiled and portrayed my story unlike my own understanding of it. I felt objectified, like I was someone else's ministry success story rather than myself. I was embarrassed to think of others reading this story and congratulating themselves because the funds they gave to support the ministry were well spent.

You Are My Other Self

In the Mayan tradition, there is a greeting, "Lak'ech Ala K'in," which can be roughly translated as "I am another yourself."

Another way of expressing its essence is "I am you, and you are me." This phrase proclaims the unity and oneness we share as human beings; it reminds us that we are inextricably connected to one another. It is a beautiful expression of mutuality and solidarity, not unlike the Hindu word "namaste," which can be translated as "The light in me honors the light in you."

Whenever I hear Father Greg Boyle of Homeboy Industries speak or when I read one of his books, I am reminded of Lak'ech Ala K'in. Father Greg is not Latinx, nor has he ever been a gang member or incarcerated, but he has lived in East Los Angeles for decades in relationship with Latinxs and specifically with former gang members, a group he affectionately refers to as "homies." Many people, Latinx or not, deeply admire his work and commitment to gang-involved youth. What most fail to recognize is that the most revolutionary aspect of his work is that he regards these young people as human beings, as friends with whom he is in close relationship and not as objects of his charity or as good fundraising stories. In fact, he often speaks of kinship to express the mutuality of his relationships with his community members.

In a similar vein, I have loved reading the books and articles of D. L. Mayfield, a writer in the Portland area who lives in community with refugees and other immigrants. Reading her book *The Myth of the American Dream*, I had no doubt that the immigrant people she writes about are her neighbors and friends. She herself is a white woman from a middle-class family and is not an immigrant, but she has chosen to make her home in an immigrant community. She and her neighbors have conversations, savor meals together, and share each other's joys and sorrows.

Mayfield, like Father Boyle, has relationships based on mutuality, not charity; for both of them, Lak'ech Ala K'in is the order of the day. They sense that we belong to one another, so they live in kinship with their neighbors, while recognizing their power and privilege and using these to advocate alongside their neighbors. I love hearing D. L. Mayfield and Father Boyle share stories about their respective neighborhoods because they are not telling others' stories—they are sharing their *own* stories with the people in their communities. Their lives are inextricably linked to their neighbors' lives, including their writing and public speaking.

In contrast, a book was released in 2020 that created quite a bit of controversy; it was called *American Dirt*. Many Latinx writers have penned commentaries on the problematic aspects of this book, whose publisher promised would humanize a "faceless brown mass."[1] Had they simply said they were publishing a romance thriller, none of us would have cared or minded, but they chose to market this book as one that would somehow contribute to advocacy for immigration policy reform and tell the stories of many Latinx immigrants. The book tells the story of a Mexican woman and her eight-year-old son, who flee their home in Acapulco, Mexico, and undertake the agonizing journey to the US borderlands after their entire family is murdered by a drug cartel.

Writer Myriam Gurba notes that among the many questionable aspects of the novel are the plethora of harmful stereotypes it perpetuates, like "the Latin lover, the suffering mother, and the stoic manchild."[2] The main character, who is a Mexican woman, also seems to know remarkably little about Mexico's culture, people, or political realities. In fact, to Gurba, the entire book is more like a melodrama, like what many white Americans *imagine* about Mexico and migration.[3] To many, the book reads like trauma fetishization, as if it is written for the purpose of allowing those in the dominant culture to consume immigrant suffering and trauma.

The problem is not that any writer would choose to write about another's identity, whether fictional or not, but *how* they choose to write about it and *what* their proximity is to the community they are writing about. The "how" and "what" bring up the ethics of telling others' stories, because there are unintended consequences of telling a story that is not your own. Mayfield and Boyle tell stories with nuance and care because they write about their friends and neighbors, not just a cause. They live in direct relationship to the people they write about, and it shows. It is important for those of us who identify as Christians to honor others in our storytelling and not exploit them. Despite our best intentions, the stories we tell may not reflect the truth of someone else's experience and may harm them.

Trauma Fetishes versus Nuanced Portrayals

As a college student majoring in English, I read Harriet Jacobs's *Incidents in the Life of a Slave Girl*, a narrative where the author recounts her experiences as a young woman enslaved in a household in the antebellum South. Jacobs tells her own story with a startling and stark realism. Her prose brings the reader fully into her narrative, with all its horrors. In particular, Jacobs narrates what it was like to experience sexual abuse and harassment at the hands of the person who enslaved her and how she struggled to mother and care for her children in that environment.

There is not a hint of sentimentality in her writing. She is a fully fleshed-out human being who does not have a single story but contains multitudes. Her narrative reveals not just trauma and suffering but resilience, strength, resistance, and resourcefulness.

The narrative documents how she experienced life as an enslaved person and how she gained freedom for herself and her children. That is how powerful telling our own stories can be—the storyteller is at the center of the process and controls the narrative; they have the power to decide what they want to share and how.

Whenever I am asked to write endorsements for books about immigration advocacy, I read them with eagerness and excitement. But I have learned that I need to read them in their entirety before I agree to give my endorsement. I find that many such books tend only to illuminate the darkest and most jarring aspects of our community's struggle. In fact, I believe many exploit immigrant pain and suffering for the white gaze. I struggle with portrayals that, in my opinion, lack nuanced descriptions because they are *mostly* suffering and trauma. It is not that the vulnerabilities of immigrant people should not be discussed or highlighted, but it should be done in balance with the whole of our stories.

Unlike Jacobs's multifaceted story of human struggle and survival, many stories I read are one-dimensional and oversimplified. I would call them the Christian *American Dirt* books. Even those of us who suffer traumas are more than just our traumas. People who are poor are more than just their poverty. And people who migrate because they feel they have no other choice are more than just suffering migrants. Storytelling must be holistic and involve a well-rounded narrative that fully humanizes and dignifies the people whose stories are being told.

Power and Consent

I am not a fundraiser or a marketing professional. And yet I know that these are important roles for any organization doing humanitarian work. The unfortunate truth is that funding is necessary to serve our neighbors if we want to be able to do it on a large scale. I once asked a fundraiser about a failed campaign, one that failed to raise both awareness *and* funding. The basic premise behind the campaign was asking donors to partner with a local leader—a person of color doing work within their own community in a developing nation to raise themselves and others out of poverty. The fundraising staff would share stories of people doing good work in their own communities and training others to do so, and the hope was that donors would want to provide more resources for these leaders. Despite having a catchy name and lots of accompanying swag, the campaign never took off.

I was perplexed. Why would people not want to give to such a wonderful model for transforming a community? Here is a situation where you do not have to bring in North American workers; you provide the funding, and the community leaders continue the work—it is efficient, cost-effective, and empowering. When I asked why the campaign failed, I was told that many donors do not want to give to local leaders; they want to *be* the heroes, the saviors. What I understood was that most donors do not want to hear stories of people serving their own communities and making a difference; they want to hear stories of human suffering that they can respond to—where they can give funding and save the day. Having someone else save the day is, evidently, not as satisfying.

Apparently, many organizations know this and adjust their communication to meet donor expectations. That is why we do not often hear stories of resilience and strength in fundraising pitches. Instead, we hear stories of human suffering and need. We hear a variation on the old television commercial that convinces us that for fifty cents a day, we can provide for a poor little girl and her whole family and save them. Alternatively, we might hear stories about how donor funding provided programming that resulted in a particular person's success story. The priority is the donor, not the person at the center of the story, because the organization's mission cannot be furthered without funding. Someone takes ownership of someone else's story, possibly with consent, and uses it to raise needed funds.

Some people do not see a problem with this approach—to them, the ends justify the means. But is that kind of storytelling ethical? How does it honor the full human complexity of the people whose stories we are sharing? How does it challenge donors' savior complexes and encourage *their* growth and transformation? Our priority should always be the person who has trusted us with their story. They should always remain at the center of our care and concern.

When we do not center the owner of the story, consent becomes a secondary concern. It may have just been assumed and not asked for, or it may have been given only to a certain extent. We do not know because that information is not usually shared with those of us who receive the story. We also do not know if the person was asked how they wanted their story shared. Some people or organizations ask for blanket consent on a piece of paper that requires a signature. While that is better than not getting consent at all, it does not account for the fact that consent must be informed and is a living process; it is ongoing, particularly in a situation where uneven power dynamics exist. Robin Wall Kimmerer describes stories as living beings that grow and develop.[4]

A person might change their mind about having their story shared at all, or they might decide that they are no longer comfortable sharing certain parts of their story. Sometimes a person who gave full enthusiastic consent might decide later that they would like their story taken down from a website or removed from donation materials. A commitment to ethical storytelling means that we give up our own power and listen to the needs and desires of the person sharing their story. This often means creating a space for those who want to share their stories and letting them tell it in their own words. They own their story and must be allowed to tell it, even if it is through a translator or in grammatically imperfect English. Obviously, this takes a lot more time, but it is what is required to respect those who share their stories with us.

We can all encourage ethical storytelling by letting others know before we share a story that we have consent to share the following story with them. We can also ask questions when we read stories on websites and donation materials and when we hear stories from the pulpit or at fundraising dinners or meetings. This is the subversive way that we can disrupt toxic and exploitive narratives. This is how we keep others and ourselves accountable and encourage environments where no one is objectified, and everyone is honored, especially those on the margins of our society.

Do No Harm

The following story is shared with my father's full consent, since our stories intersect.

When I was eighteen, I visited a church with friends for a few months. I mostly went because my friends enjoyed this community, but I usually tuned out during the pastor's meandering sermons. He went down so many rabbit trails that it was difficult to keep track of his point. One Wednesday evening service, I could have sworn that he was looking at me—every now and then he would pause, fix his gaze on me, and then give me a sympathetic smile. It was odd, but not terribly unusual or unsettling. The pastor may not have been the best preacher around, but he was a kind and grandfatherly sort of man.

As he concluded his sermon, he began walking down the aisle toward me. If I had had any doubts that he really had been looking at me, they vanished. I was sitting in the next-to-last row with my friends. When he reached me, he gave me his outstretched hand and said into his microphone for the sanctuary to hear, "We're going to pray for this young lady tonight. You see, her father is in the hospital . . ."

I do not remember what else he said but only that he shared the private details of my father's mental health struggles. I was mortified. I had not yet told the friends whom I accompanied to church, and I barely knew anyone else in this community. This was a space that lacked emotional safety for me, and he had just told everyone quite possibly the worst thing that had happened in my life after my mother's death. I felt vulnerable, violated, and exposed. I do remember that I burst into tears of humiliation and anger. I know that he intended to offer comfort, but instead he inflicted more harm. Later, I found out that the pastor was the friend of another minister my father had called from the hospital—that is how he knew. They had both violated a confidence. The pastor had neither my father's nor my consent to share that story in the form of a prayer request with the whole congregation. It was my story to share, mine and my father's.

I have long since forgiven this pastor for his clumsy attempt at offering comfort. I did so because I have also failed to do no harm in storytelling. In fact, when I first began working in immigration services, I would often tell the stories of immigrants in the Baltimore community when I spoke at churches. I have also participated in fundraising dinners and galas in which I even prepared people to share their stories before groups of donors, without making sure they had given their full enthusiastic consent and without helping them to create a well-rounded narrative that dignified them instead of just exposing their struggles for public consumption. I have shared stories from the pulpit that I later regretted. When I was overseas, I wrote my own newsletters to donors and shared stories that I did not show the people I wrote about—I did the very same thing my college ministry staff pastor had done to me, except I deceived myself into believing I did it better than she did. It is very likely that all of us have failed at one time or another fully to embrace ethical storytelling. It can be tricky since our stories so often intersect with others' stories.

Truth be told, I did not even become aware of the concept of ethical storytelling until a few years ago when I began to research it, after becoming increasingly uncomfortable at hearing others' traumatic stories shared for fundraising efforts. That is why I choose not to tell others' stories in my writing but instead to create composites of stories I hear frequently. This practice allows me to highlight issues affecting immigrants without dishonoring them and the stories they entrust to me. It allows me the freedom to change names and details and blend many stories, while protecting the privacy of the people I meet. Sometimes interviewers or other writers ask me if a particular story is true, and I respond that it is true in the way all stories are true. I regularly remind others that any story I share, other than my own, is a composite. I have also found that there are creative ways to avoid sharing others' stories by using fictional stories and published nonfiction stories. Additionally, we can use parables, folk tales, and fables because these are universal stories that belong to all of us.

Love Your Neighbor as Yourself

Stories are incredibly powerful because they engage our hearts first and then our minds. My friend Jennifer Guerra Aldana says that stories "help us make sense of what it means to love, lead, heal, live, what it means to be human. Stories have the power to be the spiritual background of our lives and they shape how we relate with each other. Each of us are a collection of stories of connection, trauma, heartache, resilience, survival and much more."[5] These are the reasons that stories are sacred; it is a privilege to hold them and be entrusted with them.

Even as we seek to raise awareness and support for immigrants and other people on the margins, the stories we tell matter. The ends do not justify the means. Dehumanizing narratives do not help our neighbors; they further harm and marginalize them. We can and should do better because funds and support can be raised with ethical storytelling. In fact, I have known fundraisers committed to this practice who are very successful.

Ethical storytelling comes down to the commandment Jesus described as one of the greatest of all: love your neighbor as yourself. In fact, it strikes me that the Mayan saying Lak'ech Ala K'in is a variation on "love your neighbor as yourself"—it is another way of expressing that we have a responsibility to one another, so we must honor each other as stories are communicated and shared. Perhaps this is the first time that you are learning about ethical storytelling. It is perfectly good and acceptable for you to start where you are. We can't do anything to change the past, but we can make different choices moving forward. As the old adage says, "Once we know better, we do better."

God of stories,

You are the God that invites us into your story. You reveal yourself to us through our stories because you journey with us from the very beginning—you know us before we know you. As bearers of your image, we are drawn to stories—the narratives we find in the Scriptures and the narratives of our friends and neighbors. Show us how to hold each other's stories as sacred and to honor them. Keep us from exploiting our immigrant neighbors by sharing their stories without permission or portraying them one-dimensionally only as people in need. Help us to become ethical storytellers who love our neighbors as ourselves. Show us how to love as you have loved us. Amen.

9

The Kin-dom Where Everyone Belongs

> God's dream is that you and I and all of us will realize that we are family, that we are made for togetherness, for goodness, and for compassion.
>
> —Desmond Tutu, *God Has a Dream*

Jesus was a pretty rude dinner guest, if you ask me. Unlike most guests, who are passively gracious and allow the host to control a gathering in their own home, Jesus takes aggressive control, sometimes even insulting the person offering him hospitality. In one instance, he dominates the conversation, finds fault with the banquet guest list, and instructs the other guests about where to sit (Luke 14:7–14). Rude! He follows these interactions with a parable about a great banquet (14:15–24).

To the original hearers of this parable, the mere mention of a wedding banquet would have evoked the coming of the kingdom of God, "the final day of celebration," often depicted in the Scriptures as a wedding banquet.[1] But contrary to social convention, Jesus tells a story about a host who invites people to his banquet, but all the original invitees turn him down, offering excuses. Justo González notes that turning down an invitation is a serious insult to the host, signaling that the guests see him as unworthy of their attendance and presence.[2]

The host is understandably angry but will not be deterred. Rather than seeking vengeance on these ungrateful guests, he does something unexpected: he sends his servant into the streets to compel people who are poor and on the margins of society to attend the banquet. The scandal of that action is lost on most twenty-first-century readers, but Luke's original audience would have understood it: "In a society of profound social distinctions, the 'unworthy' would not dream of attending a feast given by the rich and honorable. . . . Jesus is referring to people who do not expect to be invited. They feel that they do not deserve the invitation, and need to be compelled to enter."[3] In modern terms, the situation is akin to an immigrant housekeeper of an affluent employer being invited to sit at the table with the family.[4] She would have to be convinced to join her employer as an equal at the table, just as the guests in the parable have to be convinced that they are truly welcome. Pastor and writer Melissa Florer-Bixler notes that Jesus subverts the practice of a "meal-as-social-advancement" by inviting people of lower status to have the places of honor.[5]

Because there is still room at the table even after "the poor, the crippled, the blind, and the lame" join the banquet, the host sends his servant out yet again, saying, "Go out into the roads and lanes, and compel people to come in, so that my house may be filled" (14:21, 23). Bring in all the foreigners, castaways, and outsiders; this is a banquet where everyone is welcome.

A Kingdom Where Only Some Belong

When I was seven, my mother's favorite television show was *The Bionic Woman*, a science-fiction drama about a cyborg woman who has superhuman bionic powers and goes on secret government missions. It was a popular show in the late 1970s, and my mom let me watch it with her, even though I did not really understand it. I even begged her for a Bionic Woman lunchbox in second grade. Actor Lindsay Wagner, a darling of made-for-TV films in the 1980s, played the title character. Wagner was everything my family was not: she was tall and blonde, with hazel eyes, and she spoke perfect American English. My mother waited for this show each week, anticipating the new adventures of the Bionic Woman dubbed into Spanish.

When my little sister was born, my mother named her Lindsay. She said Lindsay Wagner was the most beautiful woman she had ever seen, so she wanted her youngest and last daughter to have this name. It was also an American or English name, which, to our family, gave it an air of sophistication. Because we still lived in Guatemala at that time, and Spanish is a phonetic language, none of us could pronounce Lindsay, and, truthfully, we had never even heard the name spoken out loud, so we did not know how it should sound. As a result, we ended up calling my little sister "Misha" because her middle name is Michelle.

That same year, I showed older kids on the bus my school pictures, and they said I was ugly. My innocent seven-year-old heart was wounded, and I wept all the way home and told my mother through hiccuping sobs. She reassured me and told me I was pretty. She gave me a snack, smoothed my hair, and told me not to believe those awful kids—that I was the prettiest girl in that school. Nevertheless, even at that tender age, I knew my mother thought a blonde, light-eyed woman was the most beautiful person she had ever seen, and I understood I looked nothing like this woman. Even though I, too, had a foreign name, albeit one that could be pronounced easily in Spanish, I also had brown skin, black hair, and dark eyes.

It was not hard to absorb all the aspirations toward whiteness in my family and in my Guatemalan culture. I heard my abuelita on my father's side tell stories of her Spanish father and Italian mother—she spoke with disdain about Guatemalan indigenous people, as did all my aunts and uncles on both sides of the family. My friend Bethany Rivera Molinar once noted insightfully that when white North Americans say they are Irish or German or French, they are seeking proximity to their ancestors. In contrast, when many Latinxs in the US or Latin America say they have European ancestry, we are seeking to distance ourselves from blackness and indigeneity. Proximity versus distance. It is an important distinction.

Even though our family was made up of people who were indigenous, Black, or a mixture of different races, there was always a stated clear preference for European features and white skin. As I grew up, all of my dating experiences were with white boys and, when I became an adult, white men. I could offer you any number of reasons for why that occurred—that I was raised in a white community in a suburb of west Florida, that I went to a predominantly white college and seminary, that I have been in predominantly white institutions my entire life. All those things are true, but the real reason I only dated white men is because I was raised to prefer and believe in the superiority of whiteness, and it was a harmful message I internalized.

There is a racist Latin American saying that is very popular even among Latinxs in North America: "Hay que mejorar la raza." This saying encourages Latinxs to marry and have children with someone white because of the belief that European genetic traits are superior and more beautiful and, thus, more desirable. Even though "mejorar la raza" (improve the race) is a lived reality of internalized racism for many Latinxs, this phrase is often repeated tongue in cheek, as if it is harmless and amusing. The legacy of Spanish colonialism has brainwashed our communities into thinking that being white and having European features is the only way to be beautiful. Along with racism, our communities are plagued by machismo, an extreme form of patriarchy that promotes singular ideas about what it looks like to be a man or a woman, leaving no room for any other identity or way of showing up in the world. Homophobia and transphobia are rampant in our communities.

Overt racism, prejudice, and discrimination against Black people are common and even acceptable in many Latinx communities. The racism in our communities matters because brown Latinxs are often the face of immigration activism and reform in the US, and many of us have an implicit aspiration to be white, to become secondary white people in order to access all the privileges that come with that identity. Usually, the immigration narrative is built around a brown Latinx family: a father, a mother, and their children. The parents are hard workers who contribute to the common good and simply want a better life, and they raise their children to do the same. While nothing is implicitly wrong with this narrative, it is the only one that is centered. Others are erased—namely, those of Black and LGBTQ+ immigrants, who are some of the most vulnerable immigrants in our midst. In addition, this narrative can be misleading. According to the Pew Research Center, "Starting as early as 2010, more Asian immigrants than Hispanic immigrants have arrived annually in the US, a reversal of historical trends."[6] Despite this fact, Latinx immigration and immigrants continue to be at the center of the conversation.

The immigration system is commonly understood to be unjust and outdated, broken and in need of repair. I want to challenge us to consider that it is not—the system is working just as it was designed to work: to exclude any bodies that are not white or cisgender heterosexual.

Black Immigrant Lives Matter

The last couple of years have brought a racial reckoning to the US and other places in the world. Though violence against nonwhite bodies has always existed, the invention of smartphones and their cameras have made it easier to document police brutality and other acts of aggression against Black, Indigenous, and other People of Color (BIPOC) by state actors. Miguel De La Torre emphasizes that "black lives really do not matter to white Christian society. They did not matter when Africans were brought to the Western Hemisphere to work as slaves, and they do not matter today."[7]

Whenever I give a presentation or sermon on immigration to BIPOC, I stress that the creation of the immigration system we have, the Immigration and Nationality Act (INA), coincided with the civil rights movement. This federal law ended the National Origins Formula, a racist quota system meant to prevent immigration from changing the ethnic distribution of the population.[8] The attention that the civil rights movement brought to the oppression of Black Americans also highlighted the mistreatment of nonwhite immigrants, leading to changes in the law that made it more just. We immigrants benefited from the struggle of Black Americans. Prior to this time, all immigration laws had been based on fear and the exclusion of particular ethnic or racial groups, beginning with the Chinese Exclusion Act of 1882. The INA was the first law based solely on family connections and professional skills.

Were it not for the struggles and sacrifices of Black Americans and their supporters in the civil rights movement, most immigrants of color would probably have few options under the law to remain in this country. Justice had a positive ripple effect that benefited all of us by creating more equitable and compassionate laws. No matter whom it is for, justice is good for our society. It is crucial that we stand in solidarity with one another's struggles for justice because white supremacy would have us compete with and fight one another rather than stand together.

At this time, it is especially important for us to center Black immigrants and their struggles. Few of us can forget the horrifying images from the borderlands where border patrol agents on horseback chased and seemed to be whipping Haitian asylum seekers in the summer of 2021. While no one disputes that many immigrants are mistreated, there was something different about the treatment of Haitian people, an added layer of racism. Data supports this conclusion: "Seventy-six percent of black immigrants are deported on criminal grounds, compared to 45 percent of all immigrants."[9] Essentially, Black immigrants are funneled from one harmful and unjust system to another—from immigration to criminal justice. Furthermore, Black immigrants make up 7 percent of noncitizens, but they are deported at a rate of 20 percent.[10] Black immigrants must be cautious to avoid both police and immigration enforcement, a situation that makes them more vulnerable than immigrants who are non-Black.

Black immigrants also make up a growing segment of the overall population; in 2016, they numbered 4.2 million, nearly 10 percent of the Black population in the US, a number that is expected to grow to 16.5 percent by the year 2060.[11]

Former president Trump was reported to have stated that Haitians "all have AIDS" and that Nigerians refuse to "go back to their huts" after seeing America, when he learned that Haitian and Nigerian immigrants make up 20 percent of the Black immigrants to the US.[12] While Trump's rhetoric is offensive, the founding documents and history of the US affirm his views; they indicate that anyone who is not white was never meant to be a citizen. This harmful belief has found its way inside the immigration system, making it difficult for Black immigrants to enter and stay in the country. This means that the lived experiences of Black immigrants are not unlike those of Black North Americans: "They encounter anti-black discrimination and racial prejudice because of the color of their skin. . . . They are often subject to the same risks of poverty, lack of access to quality health care or affordable housing, over-policing and increased incarceration."[13]

Our current laws and narratives are insidious because they erase and devalue Black immigrant lives, thus denigrating the image of God in them. They deny the truth that our Black immigrant neighbors have lives worthy of protection and deserving of dignity.

The Struggle of LGBTQ+ Immigrants

Each June on my social media feeds, my progressive friends are celebrating the freedom to fully be their God-given queer selves or, if they're not members of the LGBTQ+ community, to stand in solidarity with them and continue to fight for their equal rights and full inclusion in our society, including in the church. My conservative-leaning friends have chosen to focus on Immigrant Heritage Month—the biblical command to love and do justice for immigrants and the need to continue to advocate for compassionate immigration policy reform.

Rarely do I see posts that acknowledge all the ways these two observances intersect, and they do. The persecution of people because of their gender or sexual identity is not a new phenomenon; what *is* new is the growing number of asylum or refugee claims filed by LGBTQ+ individuals who are persecuted or fear persecution because of their sexual orientation or gender identity.

As you may recall from the introduction, the only difference between an asylum seeker and a refugee is *where* they apply for status—asylum seekers must be either *in* the US or present themselves *at* a US port of entry to file for this protection. Individuals who seek refugee status must apply from *outside* the US, in a country they have fled to, and must be granted the status *before* they depart for the US. Both refugees and asylum seekers flee for the same reasons: persecution or a fear of persecution for their race, religion, nationality, political opinion, or membership in a particular social group. LGBTQ+ individuals fall under the "social group" category since their sexual or gender identity is what they all share in common.

According to the United Nations Refugee Agency, in many countries, LGBTQ+ individuals, whether they are open about their sexual or gender identity or not, can experience serious human rights abuses and other forms of persecution and violence.[14] It is widely documented that they are the targets of killings; draconian laws that make their consensual sexual relations a crime; torture; gender-based violence and rape; discrimination in education, health, housing, and employment; physical attacks; unlawful detention; denial of their right to assemble; and accusations of immorality or deviance. Authorities are often unable or unwilling to protect LGBTQ+ individuals from persecution, so they are left without recourse when they suffer abuses.

When Vice President Kamala Harris visited Guatemala in the summer of 2021, she urged migrants seeking asylum not to make the journey: "Do not come. . . . I believe if you come to our border, you will be turned back."[15] Her words provoked anger, concern, and a growing feeling that the Biden administration may not be that different from the last on matters of immigration. Because asylum can only be sought at a port of entry or once an individual is in the US, her decisive words were received as discouragement from seeking out one of the few immigration possibilities for immigrants in the most vulnerable situations, like LGBTQ+ individuals.

Luz, a woman who found refuge in New Mexico, won her asylum claim based on the persecution she endured because of her lesbian identity. In her native Honduras, she was harassed at school and repeatedly raped by gang members who targeted her because of her sexual identity. To this day, Luz fears persecution and retaliation from the gang she escaped and refuses to be identified by her real name.[16] While Luz's story is unique to her, the fear and pain LGBTQ+ immigrants endure before and during their migration is universal.

My own anecdotal experience working with migrants reveals that the experiences of LGBTQ+ individuals vary greatly, but they often experience persecution in their own countries, at the hands of other migrants and local authorities in camps or on long journeys, and even once they find a safe haven in the US, particularly if they are transgender individuals.

Martin, a Cameroonian man visiting a relative in the US, seeks immigration legal counsel on an asylum petition he wishes to file on the basis of his sexual identity. He struggles to tell his story—it's common for LGBTQ+ asylum seekers to feel a great deal of shame and internalized homophobia due to their marginalization in their home countries. Essentially, no one in his family knows he is gay, not even the relative he is visiting. Martin is married to a woman, and they have three children, all of whom are very connected to his large extended family. He confesses to marrying due to societal and family pressure and to being deeply unhappy in the marriage. He understands that asylum in the US might be the only way he can live openly as a gay man, finally free of the fear of being discovered and persecuted, as he surely would be in Cameroon.

As the immigration practitioner lays out the options for Martin, he is visibly deflated. Because no one in his family or country knows of his sexual identity, he cannot prove a credible fear of persecution—this credible fear is a fundamental element in an asylum petition. One way he could acquire such proof is by telling all of his friends and family about his sexual identity and then keeping a record of their presumably negative or threatening responses. In effect, Martin would need to risk every relationship and social connection he has, including the one with the relative hosting him, in order to provide the necessary proof for the petition. That evidence of persecution, in addition to supporting documents about conditions for LGBTQ+ individuals in his country and an attorney willing to work pro bono, might be enough to win the claim.

But there are no guarantees because the granting of asylee status is unpredictable and inconsistent. According to a study conducted out of Syracuse University in 2019, 69 percent of asylum applications were denied, and asylum seekers waited an average of three years for their cases to be decided.[17] Martin decided not to pursue the petition and returned to Cameroon.

The world is still more safe and welcoming for native-born, cisgender heterosexuals.

The Kin-dom of God

The writers of the books of the Bible were likely all men who lived in a culture steeped in patriarchy. It is understandable that they used language that reflected their own patriarchal understanding of the world. Theirs was an imperialist world of male leadership and kingdoms: king, queens, princes, and princesses filled their imaginations. Kingdoms are exclusive; there are all kinds of reasons why a person might not be included in a kingdom: race, gender identity, sexuality, socioeconomic status, sex, as well as other factors.

The Bible speaks frequently of the kingdom of God, but biblical scholar and theologian Ada-María Isasi Díaz imagines it not as a hierarchical monarchy with kings at the top and peasants at the bottom but as a kin-dom, more like the parable of the banquet where all are invited and share the same table as equals. We no longer live in a world where kings rule the nations of the earth, so rather than presenting God as a monarch with absolute power, she presents a relatable, horizontal kin-dom. Her kin-dom is a more personal vision that blends the ideas of flourishing, or abundant life, with familia—the sense of familia that we have in mind when we talk about God's family and our sense of home, "of belonging and being safe, to be and become fully oneself."[18] This is the promise and joy of a new family whose members are united in the mission of Jesus.[19]

In the immigration conversation, room has been made for only one story, one vision, but I believe that God is asking us to expand that vision not in a top-down hierarchy but in a familia, where we are all kin as the family of God. In this familia, no one is excluded, and there is room for all our stories, all our backgrounds, and all our identities. I think back to the way my mother inadvertently taught me to survive in a racist and sexist world by telling me, in her own way, that life is easier for white people—that they have more opportunities and do not experience the exclusion we do. She wanted me to have access to the whole wide world, and the only way she knew how to do it was by encouraging me to assimilate to white spaces and marry into whiteness. Her only solution to help me survive these harmful systems of patriarchy and racism was to teach me to adapt to them.

I understand now that my mother did not know how to disrupt the toxic systems that create hierarchies, that divide us by race, and that exclude those who do not conform to gender or sexuality expectations. My mother could not have imagined that I would have the tools to dismantle those systems, but I do, and so do you. We no longer have to promote a vision of the world that is white, cisgender heterosexual. Isasi Díaz says, "Salvation, liberation, and the coming kin-dom of God are one and the same thing. . . . We do not make [the kin-dom] happen but [it] requires us to take responsibility for making justice a reality in our world."[20] Those who belong to the kin-dom use their resources and privilege to build a better society.

In Luke's parable of the banquet, the host and owner of the house orders his servants to invite not the people of highest status in the community but the poor, the aliens, and the vagabonds: "Then the owner of the house became angry and said to his slave, 'Go out at once into the streets and lanes of the town and bring in the poor, the crippled, the blind, and the lame.' And the slave said, 'Sir, what you ordered has been done, and there is still room.' Then the master said to the slave, 'Go out into the roads and lanes, and compel people to come in, so that my house may be filled" (Luke 14:21–23).

Many theologians believe that the second set of guests are the outcasts of Israel, and the last guests found on the roads and lanes are the Gentiles, who had not been included as a whole in Jesus's mission.[21] This parable is a kind of microcosm of God's kin-dom, since Jesus envisions a community where all kinds of different people sit side by side as equals sharing a feast: "He unsettles the unexamined. . . . We are each called out of the safety and assumption of unity with our kin, often thin and veiled, and into a new life among strangers who will become for us and for creation *la familia de Dios*."[22] Jesus is expanding the definition of family beyond blood ties and continuing a conversation started by Isaiah several hundred years earlier: "Isaiah dreams of a great banquet to be held at the end of history in which 'the Lord of hosts' spreads the banquet and serves the food of kings. It will be held on the holy mountain of the Lord and the guests will include people from all the Gentile nations. . . . It will be a glorious day of salvation."[23]

Our faith can be expansive and create room for all of us, like in Isaiah's vision. For Christians, the central act of worship is a meal, the Eucharist, in which Jesus is the host and to which all are invited, a foretaste of the ultimate divine banquet:

> On this mountain the LORD of hosts will make for all
>   peoples
>   a feast of rich food, a feast of well-aged wines,
>   of rich food filled with marrow, of well-aged wines
>   strained clear. . . .
>
> It will be said on that day,
>   Lo, this is our God; we have waited for him, so that
>   he might save us.
>   This is the LORD for whom we have waited;
>   let us be glad and rejoice in his salvation. (Isa. 25:6, 9)

God of the kin-dom,

You are the God of the great banquet, who invites all of us to the table as part of your familia. You don't delight in hierarchies and pecking orders, but we're prone to create them; we inadvertently decide some lives are more worthy than others. But that is not the kin-dom Jesus came to establish. He turned the world upside down and taught us to give without expecting to be repaid, to expect the humble places to be exalted in the end, and to accept the invitation we can't imagine is actually for us. Teach us to be part of your kin-dom. We are tired of narratives that center the most comfortable representation for the dominant culture. We want to be unsettled from our comforts and spurred to love and see as you do. We aren't waiting for your kin-dom; we want to labor with you to build it. We want justice, kinship, liberation, and belonging. Don't let our hope falter in seeking this kin-dom. Let us see you in the face of our neighbors. Amen.

Acknowledgments

Migration is a communal experience—we leave communities, and we are received into new communities. This book is also a communal work. Though writing is done through long hours of researching and writing alone, the ideas in this book began as conversations in community with friends—"en conjunto," as we say in Spanish. My comadres were part of the birthing process of this finished work. They listened to me, provided feedback and encouragement, and even disagreed at times, reminding me that it is acceptable not to take a hard stand on interpretive matters. Most of all, they let me talk about this book incessantly over the last year with the patience and kindness that only the closest friends can offer.

In particular, I am grateful to Sandy Ovalle Martínez, Jennifer Guerra Aldana, Beth Watkins, Kristy Garza Robinson, Alyssa Aldape, Aurelia Dávila-Pratt, Bethany Rivera Molinar, Kat Armas, and Alma Zaragoza-Petty. Alma kept me focused and accountable throughout my writing, and I could not have done it without her. Sandy and Jennifer discussed ideas with me and illuminated the Scriptures. I can always count on them to help me see with new eyes. And Kat, the biblical scholar of our comadrazgo, offered her support and knowledge.

I also had a great compadre who always came through with great books to read for research and theological depth—thank you, Dan Watkins. All of these friends remind me that good theology is done in community.

I also want to thank my good friends Sandy Ovalle Martínez, Candace Kim, and Laura Depp Corcorran for their unfailing love and support. Writing is very hard emotional work, and, as a single person, my emotional support and encouragement comes from my closest friends. I am grateful for these sisters who care for, celebrate with, and love me through the madness of writing and life in general.

I am also grateful for my father, Jorge Luis González Santo, and my siblings, Michelle Correia and Jorgito González, who were gracious in allowing me to tell our family stories. They read parts of this book and let me bore them by talking about it. I also recognize how much I have asked of them in discussing and reliving past experiences in our shared lives, experiences that are sometimes painful and difficult to sit with. Thank you for revisiting our stories with me.

Of course, this book would not be a book at all without my wonderful and wise agent, Rachelle Gardner. No one should have to navigate publishing without a fierce and loyal advocate like her. She believed in this book from our very first conversation. And I am eternally grateful to her for all she did to bring it to life.

In addition, I want to thank Katelyn Beaty, Melisa Blok, Erin Smith, and the entire team at Brazos Press. I wish I could help every reader understand how much work happens behind the scenes of publishing a book. Katelyn edited and revised this book over and over again to improve it and help me communicate my ideas clearly and eloquently. She met with me and was consistently patient with my concerns and questions. She provided you with the best reading experience possible.

My research and writing have been greatly facilitated by my friends and colleagues. I am grateful for the time they gave me to work on this book. I was distracted and consumed with it night and day, but they supported and prayed for me throughout the process.

Finally, I want to thank all of those people who migrate, who leave their homes in search of place, in search of safety, opportunities, and family reunification. This book is for you. Being an immigrant is a work of courage because there is so much risk in leaving and starting all over again somewhere new. You are worthy of belonging wherever you find place, just as you are.

Notes

Introduction

1. "Refugees and Asylum," United States Citizenship and Immigration Services, accessed November 28, 2021, https://www.uscis.gov/humanitarian/refugees-asylum.

Chapter 1 Strangers in a Strange Land

1. Walter Brueggemann, *Journey to the Common Good* (Louisville: Westminster John Knox, 2010), 11.
2. Brueggemann, *Journey to the Common Good*, 11 (emphasis added).
3. Brueggemann, *Journey to the Common Good*, 11.
4. Daniel José Camacho, "Moses Speaks Spanglish," *The Revealer*, November 7, 2019, https://therevealer.org/moses-speaks-spanglish/.
5. Camacho, "Moses Speaks Spanglish."
6. Jean Marie Laskas, "Bennet Omalu, Concussions, and the NFL: How One Doctor Changed Football Forever," *GQ Magazine*, September 14, 2009, https://www.gq.com/story/nfl-players-brain-dementia-study-memory-concussions.
7. Laskas, "Bennet Omalu."
8. Laskas, "Bennet Omalu."
9. Camacho, "Moses Speaks Spanglish."

Chapter 2 The Scarlet Cord and the Myth of the Good Immigrant

1. David Firth, *Including the Stranger: Foreigners in the Former Prophets* (Downers Grove, IL: IVP Academic, 2019), 20.
2. Athalya Brenner, "Wide Gaps, Narrow Escapes: I am Known as Rahab, the Broad," in *First Person: Essays in Biblical Autobiography*, ed. Philip R. Davies (Sheffield: Sheffield Academic, 2002), 47.

3. Megan McKenna, *Not Counting Women and Children: Neglected Stories from the Bible* (Maryknoll: Orbis Books, 1994), 101.

4. Cristina García-Alfonso, *Resolviendo: Narratives of Survival in the Hebrew Bible and in Cuba Today* (New York: Peter Lang, 2010), 46–47.

5. García-Alfonso, *Resolviendo*, 50.

6. García-Alfonso, *Resolviendo*, 51.

7. Firth, *Including the Stranger*, 21.

8. McKenna, *Not Counting Women and Children*, 104.

9. Shankar Vedantam (host) and Maria Cristina Garcia, "The Huddled Masses and the Myth of America," October 11, 2016, in *Hidden Brain*, produced by Maggie Penman, Chris Benderev, Jennifer Schmidt, and Renee Klahr, podcast, MP3 audio, 22:10, https://www.npr.org/2016/10/11/497091179/the-huddled-masses-and-the-myth-of-america.

10. Vedantam and Garcia, "Huddled Masses."

11. Reece Jones, *White Borders: The History of Race and Immigration in the United States from Chinese Exclusion to the Border Wall* (Boston: Beacon, 2021), 66–67.

Chapter 3 Russian for Beginners

1. Marianne Meye Thompson, "The Gospel according to John," in *The Cambridge Companion to the Gospels*, ed. Stephen C. Barton (Cambridge: Cambridge University Press, 2006), 182.

2. Graham Stanton, *The Gospels and Jesus* (Oxford: Oxford University Press, 2002), 107.

3. Stanton, *Gospels and Jesus*, 108.

4. Eduardo Galeano, "The Nobodies," in *The Book of Embraces*, trans. Cedric Belfrage (New York: Norton, 1992), 73.

5. Alexia Fernández Campbell, "Trump Described an Imaginary 'Invasion' at the Border 2 Dozen Times in the Past Year," August 7, 2019, Vox, https://www.vox.com/identities/2019/8/7/20756775/el-paso-shooting-trump-hispanic-invasion.

6. David A. Graham, "Trump Says Democrats Want Immigrants to 'Infest' the U.S.," June 19, 2018, *The Atlantic*, https://www.theatlantic.com/politics/archive/2018/06/trump-immigrants-infest/563159/.

7. Immigration and Nationality Act, title 8, chapter 12, subchapter I, §1101(42), accessed November 21, 2021, https://uscode.house.gov/view.xhtml?req=granuleid%3AUSC-prelim-title8-section1101&num=0&edition=prelim.

8. Erin Blakemore, "A Ship of Jewish Refugees Was Refused US Landing in 1939. This Was Their Fate," June 4, 2019, History, https://www.history.com/news/wwii-jewish-refugee-ship-st-louis-1939.

9. Phuc Tran, *Sigh, Gone: A Misfit's Memoir of Great Books, Punk Rock, and the Fight to Fit In* (New York: Flatiron Books, 2020), 55–56.

10. Justo González, *Three Months with Matthew* (Nashville: Abingdon, 2002), 136.

11. Anna Case-Winters, *Matthew: A Theological Commentary on the Bible* (Louisville: Westminster John Knox, 2015), 281.

Chapter 4 Reading the Bible

1. Amy-Jill Levine, *Short Stories by Jesus: The Enigmatic Parables of a Controversial Rabbi* (New York: Harper One, 2015), 3.

2. Sherwood Lingenfelter and Marvin K. Mayers, *Ministering Cross-Culturally: An Incarnational Model for Personal Relationships*, 3rd ed. (Grand Rapids: Baker Academic, 2016), 17.

3. Frantz Fanon, *The Wretched of the Earth* (London: Penguin, 1963), 32.

4. John MacArthur, "Lo Nuevo en #PorSuCausa 2016: Un Mensaje de John MacArthur" (lecture, May 5, 2016, Master's Seminary Por Su Causa Conference, https://www.youtube.com/watch?v=qiqbAa9W1TY).

5. Jonathan Merritt, "Disgraced Baptist Leader Paige Patterson Body-Shames a Woman in His Return to the Pulpit," *Washington Post*, September 14, 2018, https://www.washingtonpost.com/religion/2018/09/15/disgraced-baptist-leader-paige-patterson-body-shames-woman-his-return-pulpit/.

6. Levine, *Short Stories by Jesus*, 3.

7. Levine, *Short Stories by Jesus*, 49.

8. Levine, *Short Stories by Jesus*, 76.

Chapter 5 Mi Casa Es Su Casa

1. Richard Gardner, *Matthew*, Believers Church Bible Commentary (Scottdale, PA: Herald, 1991), 319.

2. Henri J. M. Nouwen, *With Burning Hearts: A Meditation on the Eucharistic Life* (New York: Orbis Books, 1994), 67.

3. Justo L. González, *Luke*, Belief: A Theological Commentary on the Bible (Louisville: Westminster John Knox, 2010), 278.

4. González, *Luke*, 278.

5. Kat Armas, *Abuelita Faith: What Women on the Margins Teach Us about Wisdom, Persistence, and Strength* (Grand Rapids: Brazos, 2021), 137.

6. Christine D. Pohl, *Making Room: Recovering Hospitality as a Christian Tradition* (Grand Rapids: Eerdmans, 1999), 120.

7. Pohl, *Making Room*, 18.

8. Pohl, *Making Room*, 19, 20.

9. Isaac Villegas, "The Kin-dom of Mi Abuelita," *Anabaptist World*, March 27, 2015, https://anabaptistworld.org/the-kin-dom-of-mi-abuelita/.

10. Jane D. Schaberg and Sharon H. Ringe, *Women's Bible Commentary*, 3rd ed., ed. Carol A. Newsom, Sharon H. Ringe, and Jacqueline E. Lapsely (Louisville: Westminster John Knox, 2012), 506.

Chapter 6 The Land before (Western) Time

1. Adapted from oral tradition and from Robin Wall Kimmerer, *Braiding Sweetgrass: Indigenous Wisdom, Scientific Knowledge, and the Teachings of Plants* (Minneapolis: Milkweed, 2013), 341–43.

2. Kimmerer, *Braiding Sweetgrass*, 343.

3. Kat Armas, *Abuelita Faith: What Women on the Margins Teach Us about Wisdom, Persistence, and Strength* (Grand Rapids: Brazos, 2021), 187.

4. Armas, *Abuelita Faith*, 187.

5. Clara Sue Kidwell, Homer Noley, and George E. Tinker, *A Native American Theology* (New York: Orbis Books, 2001), 35.

6. Wendell Berry, foreword to *Scripture, Culture, and Agriculture: An Agrarian Reading of the Bible*, by Ellen F. Davis (New York: Cambridge University Press, 2009), x.

7. Kidwell, Noley, and Tinker, *Native American Theology*, 136.

8. Kidwell, Noley, and Tinker, *Native American Theology*, 135.

9. Sifiso Mpofu, "A Theology of Land and Its Covenant Responsibility," in *People and Land: Decolonizing Theologies*, ed. Jione Havea (Lanham, MD: Fortress Academic, 2020), 77–87.

10. Mpofu, "Theology of Land," 79.

11. Mpofu, "Theology of Land," 79.

12. Elisabeth Malkin, "An Apology for a Guatemalan Coup, 57 Years Later," *New York Times*, October 20, 2011, https://www.nytimes.com/2011/10/21/world/americas/an-apology-for-a-guatemalan-coup-57-years-later.html?auth=link-dismiss-google1tap.

13. John M. Broder, "Clinton Offers His Apologies to Guatemala," *New York Times*, March 11, 1999, https://www.nytimes.com/1999/03/11/world/clinton-offers-his-apologies-to-guatemala.html.

14. Gemma Tulud Cruz, "When No Land on Earth Is 'Promised Land': Empire and Forced Migrants," in *People and Land: Decolonizing Theologies*, ed. Jione Havea (Lanham, MD: Fortress Academic, 2020), 43.

15. Gloria Anzaldúa, *Borderlands/La Frontera: The New Mestiza* (San Francisco: Spinsters/Aunt Lute, 1987), 19.

16. Anzaldúa, *Borderlands/La Frontera*, 25.

17. Russell Contreras, "U.S. Border Cities Again See Low Violent Crime Rates," *Axios*, October 28, 2021, https://www.axios.com/us-border-cities-low-violent-crime-rates-6f781eb0-f8f9-45c0-a41c-4b19fce33bbb.html.

18. Julian Resendiz, "Leaders Dismiss Juarez's No. 2 Ranking of World's Most Violent Cities," Border Report, June 3, 2020, https://www.borderreport.com/hot-topics/border-crime/leaders-dismiss-juarezs-no-2-ranking-of-worlds-most-violent-cities/.

19. Diana Washington Valdez, "Mexico on Trial in Murders of Women," *El Paso Times*, April 30, 2009.

20. Justin Ashworth, "Healing the Open Wound: Imagining Christian Border Ethics with Gloria Anzaldúa," *The Other Journal*, November 30, 2015, https://theotherjournal.com/2015/11/30/healing-the-open-wound-imagining-christian-border-ethics-with-gloria-anzaldua/.

21. Ashworth, "Healing the Open Wound."

22. Ashworth, "Healing the Open Wound."

23. Miguel De La Torre, *Embracing Hopelessness* (Minneapolis: Fortress, 2017), 152.

24. Makini Brice, "Protestors, Lawmaker Arrested in Senate Building Sit-in over Immigration," Reuters, June 28, 2018, https://www.reuters.com/article/us-usa-immigration-protests/protestors-lawmaker-arrested-in-senate-building-sit-in-over-immigration-idUSKBN1JO173.

25. De La Torre, *Embracing Hopelessness*, 153.

26. De La Torre, *Embracing Hopelessness*, 154.

Chapter 7 Departures

1. Sonia Shah, *The Next Great Migration: The Beauty and Terror of Life on the Move* (New York: Bloomsbury, 2020), 30.

2. Shah, *Next Great Migration*, 31.

3. Gemma Tulud Cruz, "When No Land on Earth Is 'Promised Land': Empire and Forced Migrants," in *People and Land: Decolonizing Theologies*, ed. Jione Havea (Lanham, MD: Fortress Academic, 2020), 35.

4. Cruz, "When No Land on Earth Is 'Promised Land,'" 35.

5. Justin Worland, "Your Morning Cup of Coffee Is in Danger. Can the Industry Adapt in Time?," *Time*, June 21, 2018, https://time.com/5318245/coffee-industry-climate-change/.

6. Worland, "Your Morning Cup of Coffee Is in Danger."

7. Shah, *Next Great Migration*, 10.

8. "Guatemala," Coffee Hunter, accessed October 25, 2021, https://www.coffeehunter.com/coffee-country/guatemala/.

9. Robin Wall Kimmerer, *Braiding Sweetgrass: Indigenous Wisdom, Scientific Knowledge, and the Teachings of Plants* (Minneapolis: Milkweed, 2013), 215.

10. Moisés Silva, *Philippians*, 2nd ed., Baker Exegetical Commentary on the New Testament (Grand Rapids: Baker Academic, 2005), 166.

11. Silva, *Philippians*, 166.

Chapter 8 Ethical Storytelling

1. Myriam Gurba, "Pendeja, You Ain't John Steinbeck: My Bronca with Fake-Ass Social Justice Literature," *Tropics of Meta* (blog), 2019, https://tropicsofmeta.com/2019/12/12/pendeja-you-aint-steinbeck-my-bronca-with-fake-ass-social-justice-literature/amp/#_ftn1.

2. Gurba, "Pendeja, You Ain't John Steinbeck."

3. Gurba, "Pendeja, You Ain't John Steinbeck."

4. Robin Wall Kimmerer, *Braiding Sweetgrass: Indigenous Wisdom, Scientific Knowledge, and the Teachings of Plants* (Minneapolis: Milkweed, 2013), 386.

5. Jennifer Guerra Aldana, Karen González, and Sandy Ovalle Martínez, "Ancestral Wisdom: Storytelling," October 20, 2021, in *Café with Comadres*, produced by StormMiguel Florez, podcast, MP3 audio, 29:15, https://anchor.fm/cafewithcomadres/episodes/Ancestral-Wisdom-Storytelling-e17aamn.

Chapter 9 The Kin-dom Where Everyone Belongs

1. Justo L. González, *Luke*, Belief: A Theological Commentary on the Bible (Louisville: Westminster John Knox, 2010), 179.

2. González, *Luke*, 181.

3. González, *Luke*, 181.

4. González, *Luke*, 181.

5. Melissa Florer-Bixler, *How to Have an Enemy: Righteous Anger and the Work of Peace* (Harrisonburg, VA: Herald, 2021), 113.

6. Abby Budiman, Christine Tamir, Lauren Mora, and Luis Noe-Bustamante, "Facts on U.S. Immigrants, 2018," Pew Research Center, August 20, 2020, https://www.pewresearch.org/hispanic/2020/08/20/facts-on-u-s-immigrants/.

7. Miguel De La Torre, *Embracing Hopelessness* (Minneapolis: Fortress, 2017), 127.

8. Reece Jones, *White Borders: The History of Race and Immigration in the United States from Chinese Exclusion to the Border Wall* (Boston: Beacon, 2021), 77–82.

9. Joan F. Neal, "Being Black and Immigrant in America," Center for Migration Studies, August 3, 2020, https://cmsny.org/being-black-and-immigrant-in-america/.

10. Neal, "Being Black and Immigrant in America."

11. Neal, "Being Black and Immigrant in America."

12. Jeremy Raff, "The 'Double Punishment' for Black Undocumented Immigrants," *The Atlantic*, December 30, 2017, https://www.theatlantic.com/politics/archive/2017/12/the-double-punishment-for-black-immigrants/549425/.

13. Neal, "Being Black and Immigrant in America."

14. UN Refugee Agency, "LGBTI Claims," accessed June 17, 2021, https://www.unhcr.org/en-us/lgbti-claims.html.

15. Cindy Carcamo and Andrea Castillo, "'Do Not Come': Kamala Harris' Three Words to Guatemalans Stir Debate and Backlash," *Los Angeles Times*, June 9, 2021, https://www.latimes.com/california/story/2021-06-09/kamala-harris-guatemala-immigration-speech-plays-to-voters.

16. Carcamo and Castillo, "'Do Not Come.'"

17. TRAC, "Record Number of Asylum Cases in FY 2019," TRAC Immigration, January 8, 2020, https://trac.syr.edu/immigration/reports/588/.

18. Ada María Isasi-Díaz, *La Lucha Continues: Mujerista Theology* (Maryknoll, NY: Orbis Books, 2004), 248.

19. Florer-Bixler, *How to Have an Enemy*, 118.

20. Isasi Díaz, *En La Lucha*, 53.

21. Kenneth Bailey, *Jesus through Middle Eastern Eyes: Cultural Studies in the Gospels* (Downers Grove, IL: IVP Academic, 2008), 318.

22. Florer-Bixler, *How to Have an Enemy*, 119.

23. Bailey, *Jesus through Middle Eastern Eyes*, 310.

Author Bio

Karen González is a speaker, writer, and immigrant advocate, who herself immigrated from Guatemala as a child. Karen is a former public school teacher and attended Fuller Theological Seminary, where she studied theology and missiology. She is a nonprofit professional specializing in human resources, and is the author of *The God Who Sees: Immigrants, The Bible, and the Journey to Belong* (Herald Press, 2019). She has written for *Sojourners*, *Christianity Today*, *The Christian Century*, *Christ and Pop Culture*, and others. She lives in Baltimore, Maryland, where she enjoys cooking Guatemalan food, traveling, rooting for the Dodgers, playing with her nieces, and writing while her cat Scully naps beside her.